THE MEN
COMMANDMENTS

The Bible For Blokes From
The Daddy Of Breakfast Radio

CHRISTIAN O'CONNELL

Collins

Collins
An imprint of HarperCollins Publishers W6 8JB

www.collins.co.uk

10 9 8 7 6 5 4 3 2 1

77-85 Fulham Palace Road
London

First published in 2008 by HarperCollins Publishers Ltd
This updated paperback edition published in 2009

A catalogue record for this book is available from the British Library

ISBN: 9780007284962

Designed and typeset by seagulls.net
Printed and bound in Great Britain by Clays Ltd, St Ives plc

Mixed Sources
Product group from well-managed
forests and other controlled sources
www.fsc.org Cert no. SW-COC-1806
© 1996 Forest Stewardship Council

FSC is a non-profit international organisation established to promote the
responsible management of the world's forests. Products carrying the FSC
label are independently certified to assure consumers that they come
from forests that are managed to meet the social, economic and
ecological needs of present and future generations.

Find out more about HarperCollins and the environment at
www.harpercollins.co.uk/green

To all the men.
Past, present and future.
This one's for us.

CONTENTS

Foreword by James Nesbitt – ix

Introduction – 1

I • The Man Quiz – 3
II • Rites of Passage – 11
III • The History of Men – 31
IV • Men and their Mates – 53
V • Men and Women – 83
VI • Men and Emotions – 161
VII • Hollywood: The Male Moral Compass – 183
VIII • The Future of Men – 213
IX • The Real Men First XI – 219
X • The Men Commandments – 237

Index – 290

FOREWORD
BY JAMES NESBITT

'What a piece of work is a man, how noble in reason, how infinite in faculties, in form and moving how express and admirable, in action how like an angel, in apprehension how like a god! the beauty of the world, the paragon of animals – and yet, to me, what is this quintessence of dust?'

Shakespeare knew his onions. Four hundred and one years after Hamlet so deftly defined man's complexities and insecurities, his pride and self-loathing, his capabilities for good and evil, we're none the wiser. In fact, in 2008, this is much worse. Hamlet was jammy enough to die a hero. His dad was dead, though appeared once nightly as a ghost during the summer season. His mum married his uncle, so clearly they both had to die, he had sex with his girlfriend then mistakenly stabbed and killed her father, who was hiding behind the curtain, or 'arras' as Shakespeare called it – he obviously didn't know his 'arras' from his elbow. She went mental before doing the decent thing of drowning herself before he had the 'we need to talk' nightmare, and then in his death throes after he had been pierced with a poison sword, his best mate Horatio held him in his arms and snogged him. Thus ensuring Hamlet died happy in the knowledge that he had tried everything.

But modern man. We have to live. Every day we have to live with ourselves, our partners, our children, our friends. And we don't know how to. We're scared. We're lost. How did it come to this?

How did we arrive at a situation where we spend more on grooming products than we do on beer?

Why do our mates openly discuss their feelings while our wives debate the offside trap? Why, despite our embracing of liberal modernity, do we still have no control over the groin area?

If we publicly cry more than Charles Ingalls in an average episode of *Little House on the Prairie*, does it demonstrate how in touch we are with our feminine side or do we appear weak, pathetic nonces?

Why do our children change from adoring little angels to sulky ten-year-olds, embarrassed to even breathe? And why in God's name at the age of 43 do I still suck my thumb? We need answers. Desperately.

For years women have had everyone from Mrs Beeton to Germaine Greer to Bridget Jones. Men have had no one. Until now.

Christian O'Connell looks like Jerry Seinfeld's younger brother but with bigger teeth. And has a fondness for wearing muscle tops. Not an obvious candidate for our knight in shining armour, but don't be fooled.

Our friendship is based on abuse. I listen while he abuses me. But I like to think it's borne out of love. He is as at home in the company of women as he is in the company of men. He is funny, irreverent, scathing, at times coruscating but never cruel. Very much the modern man.

He has not, however, fallen prey to the dumbing-down culture which so pervades our society. Intelligent, kind and erudite, he is a devoted husband and father. But at heart he is a man's man and is the answer to our prayers. With Christian, men can regain their identity and walk proud and tall. His wife's man, his daughter's man, his friend's man, he's my man. He's Christian O'Connell.

INTRODUCTION

Three things happened in a week that made me think I needed to write this book. First, my newspaper had a headline screaming 'The Redundant Male'. Next was my wife's sinister cackling while reading her new book, *How to Kill Your Husband*. The final insult was turning on the TV and seeing that advert for Sheilas' Wheels offering cheaper car insurance for those oh so careful women drivers. Discrimination. And during *Heartbeat*.

ENOUGH.

At no other time in history have men been so openly ridiculed – and we have only ourselves to blame. We have never been so confused about how to be a man.

Sure, there are countless books offering insights into the female condition but precious few for men. Until now.

This book is about how we are as men. When we are alone. With our mates. With women. With the TV and movie heroes that have taught us everything we know.

I would like to make it crystal clear that this is not any kind of instruction manual: none of us would read it and I wouldn't be sitting here writing it.

I

THE MAN QUIZ

This is a book for men. These days it's hard to tell who is a man and who isn't. This handy quiz may help.

1. Instructions are for:

    a. Reading

    b. Losers

2. Did you cry in *Rocky III* when Apollo died?

    a. Who is Rocky and what is Apollo?

    b. For days

3. You are invited to attend the motion picture *Sex and the City* by your other half. Do you:

    a. Happily say you'd love to go. Two and a half hours with the fab four sounds like heaven!

    b. Say, 'I'd rather rub a cheese grater across my scrotum'

**4. It is one in the morning and you return home after a
night out with your mates. Do you:**

a. Retire to bed with a warm glass of milk and an oat biscuit

b. Fire up the frying pan and start to cook despite the fact you
cannot see or stand unaided

5. A phone conversation with a mate will:

a. Go on forever sometimes!

b. Finish within a minute and in that time words will often be
replaced by a complex system of grunts, mumbles and
silences that only men understand

**6. How much time do you spend in front of the mirror
getting ready?**

a. Several minutes following an intense cleansing, toning,
exfoliating and moisturising programme

b. Less than a minute

7. The best time to call an ex is:

a. Never. Best to let bygones be bygones and move on

b. When you've had a skinful and are feeling horny

8. What are you better at recalling?

a. Birthdays, anniversaries

b. Entire lines and scenes from movies like *The Godfather*,
Police Academy 5 and anything starring Steven Seagal

9. What is the real purpose of the remote control?

a. To change the channels remotely from a distance

b. To flick around the moment the ads come on and try and see everything else that is on, but to never settle for more than 1.7 seconds on anything

10. TV detectives Starsky and Hutch and Bodie and Doyle from *The Professionals* are having a fight. Who will win?

a. Starsky and Hutch

b. Bodie and Doyle

11. You are stuck on a desert island and suddenly discover a DVD player. You have been alone for 76 days. There is only one DVD to watch: *The Godfather: Part III*. Do you:

a. Watch it

b. Grab the nearest coconut and smash the copy of *Godfather: Part III* to pieces, screaming, 'How could they do this? They ruined it!'

12. Which is better, *Star Wars* or *Harry Potter*?

a. *Harry Potter*

b. *Star Wars* because 1) Princess Leia appears in chains in a gold bikini and 2) Han Solo is a space pirate

13. When was the last time you cried?

a. Just last week when your supermarket ran out of shaved parmesan

b. During an episode of Rolf's *Animal Hospital* when a brave but sick dog died

14. You are asked 'What are you thinking?' by your partner. Do you:

a. Tell her exactly what you are thinking – you were imagining what the girl who just walked past would look like naked with you on her

b. Reply shiftily, 'Nothing'

15. The best place to relax and unwind at home is:

a. In the front room with some lovely throws and scented candles

b. In the loo under the stairs which smells but has a lock

16. A 42-inch TV is:

a. Way too big

b. Not big enough but will have to do

17. A man's position on a dance floor is:

a. On it with his partner using some steps they learnt together at a salsa class

b. Drinking at the bar, laughing at all the other men trying to dance

18. Saturday night TV is:

a. Great fun! So many exciting programmes to choose from like *Strictly Come Dancing* and *Dancing On Ice*

b. Utter shit

19. You are at a pet shop and have to choose between buying a cat or a dog. Do you:

a. Pick a cat as they are just so cute

b. Pick a dog cos they kill cats

20. You are arguing with your wife or girlfriend. Do you:

a. Work out a positive outcome, having fully understood the various issues raised

b. Apologise despite having no idea what you are sorry about

21. You notice that the loo roll is empty. Do you:

a. Replace it

b. Ignore it, not really understanding what needs to happen to replace it

22. You are lost in a car. Do you:

a. Ask for directions from a cheery local

b. Carry on driving around, insisting you are not lost and that it's somewhere round here

23. Have you ever watched more than one hour of a period drama/*America's Next Top Model*?

a. Yes

b. Sorry, I don't recognise the shows you talk of

24. You meet up with your mates in the pub. Do you talk about:

a. Your feelings

b. Who would win in a fight between James Bond and Jack Bauer

25. Do you have a pair of lucky underpants that smell and have holes?

a. Good God, no

b. Yes

26. It's your best friend's birthday. Do you:

a. Send him a birthday card and buy him a gift

b. Ignore it

27. Do you know what duck-egg blue is?

a. Sure, it's a light blue great for rooms with plenty of natural daylight

b. Colour of Man City's home kit?

28. What do you fear more?

a. Knife attack from a group of deadly ninjas

b. Man flu

29. At a barbecue, how do you know when the chicken is done?

a. When it's white throughout

b. When you say it is (despite guests throwing up and ambulances arriving)

30. What do you think of musicals?

a. Great entertainment – have seen *Les Mis* and *Cats* several times, always a blast

b. Pure evil

31. Are you over the age of 30 and wear low-slung denim around your knees? If so, please put this book down and fuck off.

If you answered 'a' to any of the above, you're not a man. Thank you for your time and interest and please place this book back on the shelf for a real man.

If you answered 'b' to any of the above, this book is for you.

I bet some of the questions made you think, even hesitate, before answering. We are confused, aren't we? We don't know what we are supposed to be any more. I don't know how to change the wheel on my car. My dad does, though. I'd just get the AA out. We use moisturisers and eat sandwiches with rocket in. What's happening to us?

I guess it would make sense to start this book at the beginning. Our rites of passage.

II

RITES OF PASSAGE

On the journey through life we pass through various experiences that shape who we are. The boy becomes the man. Or more likely the boy stays the boy but buys a house, gets married and has kids, all the time wondering when is he going to grow up and stop laughing when people fall over.

But what are the key moments in a young man's life and development?

PARENTS

Whether it's informing you that eating apple core will make trees grow out of your ears or that playing with yourself will turn you blind, these people shape us into what we become. Be it a serial killer or an MP – it's all their fault.

Actually, it's our dad who gives us the first impression of what a man is and does. My dad was very loving and he instilled a great sense of 'you can do anything in life if you work hard enough' in me. He was and still is nuts.

The best story to illustrate this is how we dealt with the death of my younger sister's cat. Well, actually, it was the second cat death in our family. The first died after my dad accidentally left it out one night. In the snow. Sadly this was before Ray Mears and Bear Grylls so poor Henry didn't know how to construct a rudimentary bivouac for shelter.

The second one, a beloved tabby cat called Pepper, passed away in less extreme circumstances. My sister was understandably upset but my dad assured her that he would be on his way to Cat Heaven and he would take care of his burial. What I'm about to tell you is beyond belief – but please don't judge my dad as he is made from the same man genes as us all. Having been promised a decent cat send-off for poor beloved Pepper, my sister came running into the house in floods of tears. Hysterical. She claimed in her emotional state to have seen 'my Pepper on a skip'.

Now it's not unknown for the grief-stricken to see visions of the recently departed. That's what must have happened here. Or so I thought. My dad calmed her down and asked me to help him with something. He quietly told me we needed to move the body.

Sorry, Dad? The body?

You see, my dad had deposited poor old Pepper, the family cat, on the neighbour's skip. Hey, who hasn't dumped some carpet underlay or old paint tins in a neighbour's skip late at night? But a dead pet? He hadn't even made an attempt to cover it with anything! So now he was getting his son in on his deception, and I was loving it. Both father and son bonded and giggled as poor old Pepper was lifted off the skip and taken elsewhere. Then my dad calmly told my sister we had just checked the skip and there was no cat body. Go see for yourself, he urged her. She checked it and agreed. I had learnt a valuable lesson: men lie.

Then there was the time he tried to landscape the garden on the cheap by doing it himself. He hired this beast of a thing called a rotavator. He tried to steer it one way and it flung him over the neighbour's fence. All I saw was this runaway rotavator, Dad-less, and then I heard a word I hadn't heard before – 'FUCKER!' – as my dad popped up the other side of our neighbour's fence, leapt back over and began to chase after it. Shirtless, wearing only, of course, his magical Dad Pants.

I learnt another valuable lesson. Men are funny. Funny peculiar. Oh, and another lesson: always hire a rotavator with an automatic cut-off switch.

SCHOOL DAYS

When I think of my school days, I physically wince. It's the flashbacks of brand new shoes in September, which had no give in them until March the next year, at which point it was time for a new pair of Clarks Commandos. In your early school days your mum dresses you... but then something called puberty happens.

In men puberty lasts until they die.

So many changes happen to the young man. First come the little acts of rebellion in your school uniform. You don't want your mum's big fat Windsor knot in your tie – I was at school in the eighties so it was now a slim jim. Or you tucked it away into your shirt. Then you wanted to wear Stay Press trousers. You couldn't hope to get a girl's attention without Stay Press.

Then it was the looking at girls differently. Very differently. Getting these funny feelings you didn't really understand. You used to be happy to stare out of the window during lessons, praying for excitement like a stray dog running into the playground. Now you stared at bras and tried to work out who had one and who didn't. Oh, and the teachers' breasts.

Puberty is hard on a young man. How do you cope with getting unwanted and embarrassing erections in the middle of a history lesson about the Great Fire of London? They were either unwanted or I was getting the horn from all that fire talk. It was even worse during PE. The girls in PE skirts, getting cheap thrills coming down the ropes. Me and my grubby mates suddenly taking a very keen interest in netball lessons. Happy days. I remember this girl at school who was very attractive, totally aware of it and a terrible tease. During a squash lesson, she was playing our teacher and we were all told to watch as he demonstrated his court technique. She had conveniently forgotten her outfit so was playing in little more than her bra and knickers. With her pert breasts bouncing up and down. It was too much not only for the boys leering down at the court action but also the teacher. He started to show a boner. I helpfully and loudly pointed this out, thinking it was part of his 'court' technique, and everyone started shouting, 'MR _____'S (name deleted here as he was a good teacher and I feel bad about humiliating him, but not that bad as it was funny) GOT A BONER.' We were ordered to go and get changed immediately and wait in the school minibus. When he got into the minibus to take us back to school he told me to get out and walk. I had learnt another lesson. Never ever laugh at another man's erection.

PE

It was during the hell of PE and games that I got my first real sense of rejection. At school you just want to be part of the gang, to have some sense of belonging. You don't want to be an outsider. You want to be in the school football team. My problem was that I was very bad at football. My toe punt had killed several kids and therefore I never got picked. At break time I was always last – chosen after the asthmatic kid, the fat kid with tits and the kid with a sticking plaster over one of the lenses of his glasses. I don't think I've ever got over the feeling of rejection of not making the school football team and maybe it's that that made me want to sit in a little room each morning talking crap between songs. I am still looking for the approval the PE teacher never gave me. All the awards, they don't help the pain.

While we are on the subject,
what's the deal with PE teachers?
Psychos. Why did they hang around the showers checking
we were going in naked? And, of course, like every other school,
there was this kid who hit puberty at eleven and had an enormous
cock that quite obviously scared/fascinated the PE teachers. I
never understood why the PE teacher had his own office. All that
was in there were tennis rackets and porn mags, or so my young
fertile mind would imagine. Watching too many *Porky's* films
polluted my mind.

SCHOOL MUSICALS

After the sporting rejection I decided maybe the world of school
entertainment would prove to be my calling. So I auditioned for
the school production of *Bugsy Malone*. With the promise of
after-school rehearsals (mainly with girls), I was on to a winner.
It would also keep me away from my penis and my masturbation
habit, which was threatening to overtake my life.

The only small obstacle in my way was the audition. Simple.
Sing to the Head of Music any song you wanted. As a huge Elvis
Presley fan, I went for 'Blue Suede Shoes'. I now regret this.
What justice could a spotty 13-year-old with a breaking voice do
to The King?

I was to stand behind the music teacher - 'Just call me Dave' -
while he accompanied my powerhouse of a performance on the
piano. I set off at a blistering pace full of vim and vigour that The
King himself would have been proud of. This was soon derailed
by the shaking shoulders and head of 'Just call me Dave'. At first I

thought he was getting lost in the powerful vocal performance from yours truly, giving it some Jerry Lee Lewis at the piano. But no, he was shaking with barely concealed laughter. At me. And in a way at Elvis. I kept going until the end like a pro and quickly made my excuses and left. (Hey, 'Dave', I hope you're living alone in rented accommodation now while I talk to – no, enthral – an audience of 17 each morning. FUCK you!)

The next day the cast list went up on the school noticeboard by the staff room where we all thought the teachers had orgies. I was cast. As Knuckles. Who was a heavy. Cool, I thought, they cast me as a hard man due to my rugged presence. Like the future man I would become, I was developing a keen sense of denial and the ability to kid myself. I slowly realised Knuckles was also a mute. I learnt another valuable lesson. Only gay boys do school musicals.

DINNER LADIES

It's at school we get our first taste of authority figures. At primary school (or whatever it's called now) there was that most terrifying form of humanity: the dinner lady. No word of a lie, I once saw one slap an unruly kid who was having a really bad Brussel sprout tantrum and had made the mistake of kicking a dinner lady in the shins. The resulting smack lifted him off his feet and sent him through the air. I heard that those Chinese nutjobs who guarded the Olympic flame when it came to London were trained by dinner ladies.

OF BED SHEETS AND SNAIL TRAILS

It's also at school that our young man minds first get filled with the low background chatter of sex. A lot. As little boys our willies are things of fascination, and they remain that for the rest of our lives. With puberty, the fascination becomes an obsession. Most men grow out of this – unless you're an MP or a professional footballer.

Its size, measuring it, playing with it. Our lives revolve around our own special friend. I remember an assembly which was all about sexual reproduction. The girls were told all about the changes they would be going through, and us boys got cheap thrills at the slides of breasts in bras. Then the woodwork teacher walked out and started telling us, and I'm not making this up, how to correctly measure your penis. The woodwork teacher. He said, as only a man could, that looking down at your penis was an inaccurate way to determine its length due to depth perception. A tape measure was best. I was now trying to work out how I was going to smuggle my mum's tape measure out of her sewing kit.

'What do you need that for, darling?'

'Just going to measure my cock.'

'OK, don't forget your tea's almost ready.'

My journey into self-pleasure coincided with something that I now look back on as some kind of cruel trick played by my parents. They had done my bedroom out and pretty damn cool it looked too. The problem was my bed sheets. They were black.

Well, black with what resembled snail trails everywhere. I remember my mum's look of surprise as I started to do my own washing – but just the bed sheet. I almost had to get help to break it in half to get it in the washing machine. The evidence, trail of evidence, was there for all to see, and it prompted my mum to say ominously, 'Your dad's going to have a chat with you about all that.' Yes, it was time to have the birds and bees chat. Oh God.

It was a very brief chat, short on detail and anything of any use. Just a 'You know about it all, do you?' and that I was to use a condom. Which I was already. For making water bombs. Did they have any other use?

Thankfully, one of the kids at my school had the business acumen of a young Sir Alan Sugar and had started selling pornographic magazines. Where he got them from we never knew. If you were really lucky, though, you would find a free one in a hedge. You don't seem to see this so much any more. I often wondered how this started. Was it someone's remote storage place? Were they hidden there by the publishers, trying to get us hooked? No one knows. These days hedges have been replaced by the internet.

I did eventually have to buy one (the hedge supply had dried up) and I have to be honest and say it actually scared me. The nudity and images were too much too soon for me and I disposed of it in the neighbour's hedge. A lovely old man lived there with his wife, and he did have a heart attack shortly after my hedge gift.

Was my copy of *Razzle* (with its '3 Bum Special' feature) to blame in any way?

Things went into hormonal overdrive every Friday night with a new TV series called *Dempsey and Makepeace*. Move aside *The A Team* and *The Rockford Files*, Glynis Barber has arrived! By now I had a TV in my room and I would say good night to my parents a full ten minutes before it started – much to their surprise. What kid when finally allowed to stay up late goes to bed early?

Saying I was tired and needed to go to bed, I would leg it upstairs to get ready. I needn't go any further other than to say that the TV needed a good wipe down on a Saturday morning. Those snails had been on the move again...

SCHOOL DISCOS

I think our fear of the dance floor stems directly from the experiences at the school disco. I'm sure the French spend their youth grinding up against each other to soulful ballads but in my experience all you used to do was skid on to your knees across the polished gym floor, push the nerds into the girls and pogo around like an idiot to Adam and the Ants.

When Phyllis Nelson's 'Move Closer' came on, it was simply a signal for me to take a break from the action and shovel more crisps, E numbers and Panda Pops down my throat. If you did get lucky and find a girl actually willing to dance with you, her mere physical presence in your postcode brought instant arousal. I think that's another reason why men are so rubbish at dancing.

Trying to dance while hiding a massive diamond cutter in your trousers can be a very traumatic process. I also remember a very dodgy teacher 'insisting' he had a slow dance with all the school hotties. I think it was this that first got me thinking that teaching might be the career for me.

SATURDAY JOBS

Saturday jobs are the first taste we get of the dullness of paid work. And wearing an ill-fitting polyester uniform. But you learn valuable lessons. Firstly, that people who work in management are often from the shallow end of the gene pool. A gene pool someone may have pissed in. Secondly, you learn the importance of skiving and that if you're given a good job to do, you make it last as long as is humanly possible.

I was lucky in that after a few jobs waiting tables and washing up, I was headhunted from the groceries aisle of Sainsbury's by Marks and Spencer. That's not strictly true, although I did work on the groceries aisle at Sainsbury's. There was a stunning girl who worked on the till who I was besotted with. My affections were sadly never returned. I guess it's hard to be won over by a streak of piss in a three-quarter-length brown overall and matching Stay Press brown pants. That were three inches too short. In movies, a mental person is usually the one wearing pants that are too short for him.

One of my best mates, Kevin, and I both managed to get jobs at Marks and Spencer. This was the place to work as they paid well and had a great canteen. That and the fact they had a lingerie section you could gawp at.

What happened next was the stuff of novels and movies. Two friends enter the same institution but are given vastly different jobs and their lives and fortunes change for ever. I was put straight on the tills. The best gig. Ten items or less. I became something of a hotshot, famed for my rapid scanning technique. The 'Maverick' of Winchester Marks and Spencer. My friend Kevin, my 'Goose', however, was put on trolley collection. This is a role usually reserved for people who enjoy licking windows. He was not happy about it. I was.

Sadly my time there came to an end as my Saturday hangovers got worse. Most mornings I would excuse myself to the store sick bay to sleep off the effects of a night on the cheap cider. Or the '24-hour flu bug', as I told them. Things really came to a head one Saturday morning when I didn't turn up and went to a big party for the weekend instead. The personnel department feared the worst – that I'd suffered an accident – and called my home. (I should point out here that I used to ride my motorbike into work. When I say 'motorbike' I mean one of those 50cc hairdryers on wheels.) My younger sister happily told them where I really was.

Upon returning to work the following Saturday, I was quizzed by the personnel lady and I'm afraid to say a very bad lie came out. I told her I had been at a beloved aunt's funeral. Dabbing my eyes in a performance De Niro would have been proud of, I was thrown off when she then said, 'That's odd because when we called you your sister told us you were headed to a party.'

I reflected momentarily on this before replying. To this day I'm ashamed of this even more shocking lie: 'My sister, yes, she has something wrong with her... Her brain... Retarded... Very sad.' The poor woman in personnel looked at me with a mixture of utter disgust and pity. Pity, I guess, about what would become of a young man who could lie in such a fashion. A DJ, obviously.

UNDERAGE DRINKING

Just as my experience of the working world was forming, so was my enjoyment of getting drunk with my mates and then trying to get laid. In my peer group I looked the oldest because I had bum fluff. Who can forget bum fluff? Wispy growths of hair around your chin that you thought made you look like Clint Eastwood in *The Good, the Bad and the Ugly*. The plain truth was you just looked silly

Whether you had bum fluff or not, there was one thing all teenagers needed: fake ID. You could usually get your fake ID from someone's older brother who was like Donald Pleasance in *The Great Escape* – 'The Forger'. He'd make them on his BBC Micro or Commodore 64. The standard was pretty poor.

Getting the booze was by two routes, both with their own hazards: the off licence or the pub.

Let's look at the off licence first. This needed planning. Any hormonal wobble in the not consistently broken voice could jeopardise the whole mission and it would be no White Lightning or Merrydown cider for you. I remember once going in and successfully buying six litres of cider and two cans of tramp juice (Special Brew as a kind of a chaser in the unlikely event any ladies joined us) then going four feet round the corner to where everyone else was lying in wait for the goods. As I was dishing out the stash, the owner walked out and rumbled us. Showing the morals of any true businessman, he asked if all this booze – six litres of industrial-strength cider and two cans of Special Brew – was for me. Yes, I replied, very high-pitched. He then walked away, happy with his rigorous spot check. Within the hour I was vomiting by a canal having also wet myself.

I'm now going to tell you a story that my dad brings up at all family get-togethers. It involves the two pillars of teenage rites of passage: underage boozing and trying to impress girls. The story goes like this: I had been invited with my mates to a party at someone's house whose parents were away. I knew it was in a posh area so I thought I would upgrade my poison to show my class: I took a bottle of red wine. Which I drank from the bottle. I also thought the girls would be impressed if I drank it really quick. This I did and I was pretty sure I was the very life and soul of the party. Then it all started to get a bit fuzzy. The sweating started first, and then the room started to spin. I ran, knocking over things on sideboards, to the toilet. The night was not going as I had hoped but worse was yet to come. My friends saw my rapidly deteriorating state and called my dad to come and get me.

They carried me to the comfort of the kerb outside, which is where my dad found me when he pulled up in his brand new car. A Ford Escort he was so proud of. The first brand new family car we'd ever had. He never even uttered an angry word as I was gingerly put in the front seat and my two giggling mates got in the back. We set off. This is where the really bad thing happened.

The motion was not good for me. I began retching. 'Wind the window down if you're going to be sick,' my dad urged. My motor skills weren't up to that and I threw up all over the dashboard, gear stick, even my dad. My mates in the back couldn't hide their laughter. My dad was now beginning to retch but still managed to drive the incredible exploding son home. He had his jacket pulled over his mouth in an attempt to escape the dreadful smell next to him. In his brand new car. My memory is hazy as to the events that followed. What I do clearly remember is waking up the next day.

First thing I felt was my throat. It was on fire. My nose was blocked. But that was nothing to what came next. Into my consciousness in a drip-drip manner came the memory of what had happened last night. In my dad's brand new car. Holy shit. I then realised there was a very strong smell of disinfectant in the house. Some late-night cleaning had happened. I didn't want to leave my bedroom.

I hobbled downstairs to see my mum. She said nothing – just nodded in the direction of my old man reading his Sunday paper. Could this be any worse? I told my dad how very sorry I was and made the promise I am still making 20 years later – that I would never get in a state like that ever again. He summoned up his dad wisdom and said quietly, 'Bollocks.'

I was stunned. 'Sorry?' I said.

He then explained that of course I would do something like that again, and asked what had happened. I told him about the red wine and the rapid drinking method of seduction. He said, and I remember it to this day, 'Son, you will do many more stupid things to get your dick wet.' I had never heard that expression before and still haven't to this day. But his words were so true.

My mum and my sister were not so understanding. For the next few weeks no one could sit in the front passenger seat because of the stench of chunder. The seat was permanently stained in a V-shape where my legs had been. Weeks later little bits of dried pasta could still be found.

I said earlier there were two ways of getting booze. The other way was pubs. For some reason, we always went into pubs in groups of about 30. It was strength in numbers, I think; the theory being that it would take too long to check our entire group's fake ID. In my local pubs, checking our age extended to 'You old enough to be drinking in here?' A chorus of various pitched 'Yeahs' would mean lagers all round. We were now men. Drinking with other men. But with poor facial hair.

VIRGINITY

To men, young men, virginity is something you want to get rid of ASAP. To young ladies it's something to cherish. The frigid ones, anyway.

I'm not going to say too much about the losing of my cherry as gentlemen never tell. That and the fact I was very bad. All I can say was that it was on an overseas holiday with my family. I took off my espadrilles a boy and put them on again a man. The whole encounter lasted no more than a few minutes. And that included the taxi back to hers.

At school there were so many rumours and myths surrounding sex. For a while I was seriously led to believe that if you had sex with someone and you were wearing a Swatch watch (remember those?) then they wouldn't get pregnant. This may be why I have two small children.

THE END OF FIRST LOVE

Underage drinking, losing your cherry, getting and spending your first pay cheque. You think these mark you as a man. They don't. Having your heart broken for the first time does.

I remember when I was first properly dumped. 1986. Man, it hurt. Mainly the pain from trying to break the vinyl single of 'our song'. You cannot simply snap vinyl. You have to bend it several ways. It takes ages. Which lessens the thing, really.

My mind was tormented. When would I ever be able to see and touch a pair of breasts again? So many happy memories of me staring at the very things Steven Williams had shown me in that magazine that time. Makepeace had a pair of these too. Now I was girlfriend-less but more importantly boobless. Time to play really depressing music over and over again until my mum told me to get outside in the sun and open my curtains.

I needed to heal my aching heart. My parents needed me to stop moping. It was decided I should join a club or society. My mum had heard from a friend with a very serious and polite son that he was enjoying the St John's Ambulance Brigade. So I was made to go along. Stop laughing. We are the people who are first on the scene of major disasters at fêtes with some weak lemon barley squash. I once saved a man's life – he had severed an arm at a banger racing meet – with weak lemon barley squash.

Every Friday evening in a damp and smelly church hall, I and some other teenage boys would meet up and practise first aid. The best bit was French-kissing Annie. That's Anatomic Annie, the rubber doll we were supposed to be honing our resuscitation skills on. The next girl I kissed benefited from the time I spent perfecting my snogging. I pinched her nose and blew into her mouth.

There were also girls in St John's Ambulance Brigade and we would get to see them at the various public events we attended. I was something of a rebel among my fellow Johners by wearing

Stay Press jeans as part of my uniform. This was not standard issue, I need you to know. This Fonze-like coolness was countered by being forced to wear a beret. I looked like Frank Spencer. However, at one memorable school fête, during a lull in field casualties being brought in from the coconut shy, I somehow managed to start getting off with a girl. In the back of the ambulance.

With her grey uniform, black tights and all that triangle bandage play, it was too much for me. I casually removed my beret, took off my white handbag that contained my first aid kit (bandage, safety pin, lemon barley squash and some Chewits – the Chewits were for me, gotta chew something while saving lives) and the ambulance was soon rocking. We were discovered and I was asked to leave the brigade. I was made up. It was the first time I'd had my hand up a girl's skirt. The Stay Presses had worked a treat.

Over the next few decades, various rites of passage would happen to us. Moving in with someone. Them moving virtually all your stuff into the nearest bin to allow more space for all their stuff. Owning your first home. Having your first mental breakdown trying to buy that first home. Attempting your first flat-pack. Surprising yourself with the number of swear words you know while building that flat-pack.

Whatever the rites of passage, men are tested – and when that testing comes you can bet we will rise to the occasion. And do something odd. The boy in the Stay Presses is now the man who still carries a small quantity of weak lemon barley squash just in case.

III

THE HISTORY OF MEN

THE IMPORTANCE OF HISTORY

Men love history. You've only got to look at the hordes of strange men who hang around the Military History section at Waterstones to realise this. Not too many around the Homes and Interiors section or Wellbeing, but history? We *love* history. In most *Sopranos* episodes, big Tony Soprano was enjoying whatever was on the History Channel. By now most areas and subjects of history have been covered. You could say some have been over-covered. I mean, how many more books about Nazi Germany can be written? I liked Stalingrad as much as the next man but when they start bringing out books like *What Hitler Had for His Tea: Volume III: Wednesday* or *An MTV Cribs Special at Adolf's Bunker* we know the market is saturated.

This chapter is a fresh look at the great moments in man history. All told from the point of view of a man whose brain is slightly addled from overdosing on butterscotch Angel Delight as a kid. My filter will focus on man history's greatest hits. Sure, everybody knows who Albert Einstein is. He invented the theory of relativity. He also had great inventor hair. What the hell does it mean, though? It teaches us nothing about ourselves as men. There is a statue of Albert Einstein standing outside the National Academy of Sciences in Washington, DC. It should be the man who invented the remote control. Or a statue of Percy Spencer. You don't know who Percy Spencer is, do you? This is exactly what I'm talking about.

Well, he is in my opinion a greater scientist than Einstein. This is because Percy Spencer was the inventor of the microwave oven. His story is the epitome of what men's history should be about. Yes, other scientists may have worked out ways to provide clean water for millions of people and that's great, but every man should have a special place in their heart for Professor Spencer. He has provided millions of men with an amazing gift. The ability to be able to make an inedible meal within 30 seconds. Plus he accidentally discovered the technology while he was trying to blow stuff up.

As a former employee of the US Navy, Spencer was trying to refine and produce very powerful microwaves for use by American fighter planes – I presume so the pilots could heat food in their cockpits and enjoy a nice ham and cheese toastie while warmongering.

One day he accidentally strayed into the path of these rays and noticed that the peanut chocolate bar in his pocket had melted. He realised that these rays could cook things. But the brilliance of Spencer was that he didn't decide to go down the route of trying to turn his discovery into a horrible death ray. Oh no. He decided to use it for *male emancipation.*

With the advent of the microwave we no longer had to make a hash of trying to cook a meal with proper ingredients and four hours' cooking time. We no longer had to suffer in silence eating beans on soggy toast, because now we had a machine that could nuke a meal in 30 seconds and we wouldn't have to miss any of the football on the television.

OUT OF THE SEA

If we're going to do this thing properly we should take our starting point as the moment we crawled out of the sea. This one's a no-brainer. We all know men hate the sea. Sure, we'll swim in it, we'll hang around on the beach and look at it, but *live in it?* No way.

You've only got to look at any man on holiday whining about all the dried saltwater on his back and the fact that his soggy shorts are making his arse itchy to realise, men + sea isn't going to be a long-term deal. Our genitals don't like it either. Shrinkage happens, as Jerry Seinfeld told us.

So at some point around 315 million years ago we decided we'd had enough. That and one of us spotted a prehistoric babe in swimwear and someone selling cheap counterfeit watches and to the beach it was, baby!

For the next 314 million years or so we ambled about on the earth splitting into hundreds and thousands of species. This makes sense. Men aren't the best at staying together; we like to drift off as something catches our eye. You often see women frantically looking for their boyfriends and husbands in shopping centres only to find them safe and well staring at the widescreen TVs or fondling gadgets. I'm always losing my wife at the supermarket. Maybe they need a desk for Lost Men to go to.

This is a store announcement. Has anyone lost the following men: Steve, Bob and Gary? If these men are yours please come and collect them from the Lost Man Desk...

Without wishing to sound dismissive of this period, not much really happened. What man couldn't enjoy wasting 314 million years doing fuck all? Man heaven.

Obviously I'm not counting the dinosaurs – they were very exciting – but this book isn't called *The Dinosaur Commandments* (that's the next one). In fact, the most exciting thing that happened to mankind during this long era was that around 100 million years ago, we reached a crossroads in our evolution.

MOUSE OR MONKEY?

We had the choice to become monkeys or mice. That's right, it was a simple case of would we rather be mice or monkeys? And who doesn't love a monkey? Think of how much as kids we loved the PG Tips adverts with the piano-moving chimps. Arguably the greatest advertising campaign ever. Chimp removal men. Genius.

We rightly chose the path of monkey and modern man avoided the prospect of a tail and buck teeth (apart from the inhabitants of certain parts of Norfolk).

Then after a couple of 100,000 years (men don't like to rush anything, it's all in the preparation) we worked out it would be easier to walk on our hind legs and use sticks to smash things up. This was made possible by another huge evolutional leap: *the opposable thumb*. Evolutionary scientists will tell you that this development was important because it enabled us to pick up wood, make tools and hold things. This is all true, but thumbs were a much more important development in man history. Now for the first time since the universe began, we could give each other the thumbs-up.

No talking, no elaborate rituals, just a simple thumbs-up. The thumbs-up sign of course reached its zenith in the mid-twentieth century with the advent of *Happy Days* and the invention of the Fonzie double thumbs-up. The thumbs aloft was then ruined for ever by Radio One DJs and Sir Paul McCartney.

CIVILISATION

The primitive cave paintings of Trois-Frères in southern France contain some of the finest preserved examples of prehistoric art. Roughly 311 million years after crawling out of the primordial ooze, man decided to chronicle his achievements by taking some animal blood and tree sap and painting on the walls of his cave. If they hadn't there would have been no Tony Hart, *Rolf's Cartoon Club* or Neil Buchanan's *Art Attack*. It's not even worth thinking about. Though Morph was ruined when they brought in that plasticine wanker Chas.

What did these brave Neanderthals depict in the early paintings? Their battle against rival tribes? The taming of fire? A list of all the woolly mammoths they had hunted and killed? Nope. They simply drew a massive penis. Really. It says a lot about the psyche of man that you can travel back to the cradle of humanity and the first tentative steps towards civilisation and literally find a willy scrawled across it. You can imagine one caveman spending hours painting a hunting scene, then going for a wee and coming back to find a big cock and balls scrawled across his hard work and his mates in the corner sniggering. It's reassuring to know that almost 15,000 years later we've come full circle from drawing penises in French caves to drawing the very same penises on bakers' heads in French language textbooks at school.

MAN'S FIRST LOVE

It was around about this time that man started the most significant relationship of the millennia. Fire.

We can never truly know how man was introduced to fire but we know that it was definitely love at first sight. However, it's strange that almost 10,000 years later we still can't cook a piece of chicken on a barbecue without giving everybody food poisoning.

SOMETHING WAY MORE IMPORTANT THAN JUST A WHEEL

Imagine the scene for a moment. A prehistoric man is strolling through the forest and he sees a load of ripened apples that have fallen off a tree. It's summer and they've begun to rot. Most of the men walking by are thinking, Urgh, look at that manky rotten fruit, better steer well clear of that, but one guy stops and makes a scientific link that happens perhaps once in any generation.

What if we can use that rotten fruit to get off our faces and shout really loudly and repeat the same story and joke over and over again and then fall over and vomit? Wouldn't that be great?

Soon he's invented rudimentary alcohol and he's churning out the precursor to Stella Artois.

STAGGER LIKE AN EGYPTIAN

Egyptians may have been the first real beer monsters. In Egyptian society they invented beer before they invented bread. That's right, beer came before bread.

Egyptians believed beer was invented by one of their most powerful gods: Osiris. Of course they did. Who knows how strong that stuff must have been. Imagine a deity who says, 'Forget continents, seas and mountains, the first thing on my list to create is beer. Let's get the party started!' This explains why the Egyptians built so much weird stuff for no good reason. They were pissed most of the time.

'Oh wise Tutankhamun, we have finished your grand Pyramids, what would you like us to do next?'

'Build me a massive statue with a... dog's head... Yeah, a dog's head. And then build me a sphinx.'

'What is a sphinx, oh lord?'

'It's a lion with a woman's head... Urggh, I think I'm going to be sick.'

The Egyptians, in their drunken haze, were soon overtaken by the new boys on the civilisation block, the Greeks. Mathematics, astronomy, medicine, and a nice salad. They also invented one of the most important things in man history. Organised sport. The Olympics.

Legend has it that the games were instituted after Hercules won a foot race at the Greek city of Olympia and then decreed that the race should be re-run every four years. But in reality, you put enough men together in one place and sooner or later they'll decide to challenge each other to some contest or other. The

Olympic Games of yesteryear bore no resemblance to the games of today, though. Mainly because the ancient Greeks hadn't invented anabolic steroids.

MAN'S GREATEST FEAR

By the first century BC it was the Romans' turn to take centre stage. Julius Caesar was the first dictator of the Roman Empire and the conqueror of Britain. One thing not everybody knows is that he was also one of the first men to tackle one of the largest problems known to men. Hair loss.

Back then, there wasn't much you could do about it. Even though wigs did exist, they were no way as near to the quality of those atop Sir Elton John's head. Even the scourge of the Roman Empire Hannibal was reputed to have worn a wig into battle against the Romans. History records that he lost the confidence of his men.

It must have been hard to inspire men to following you into a dangerous battle if they were constantly shouting 'OY WIGGY' at you behind your back. Caesar, however, came up with a novel solution. He invented the comb-over. One of the greatest historians of the era, Plutarch, recorded this at the time, but he never said whether or not it flapped about in the wind. As the most powerful man in the world, his courtiers and lackeys would have been unable to mention it. Which maybe explains why today a lot of men truly believe comb-overs are completely invisible to the naked eye.

IT'S ROUND HERE SOMEWHERE

They say all roads lead to Rome and it's true because they were the first civilisation to realise that men get lost very easily. They built miles of nice long, straight, even roads. It would seriously affect their reputation as the most fearsome army in the world if on their way to fight the Celts they had to stop and ask for directions from the Gauls.

THE TUDOR SMACKDOWN

Let's race forward to 1509 when one of the most memorable kings of England came to the throne. Henry VIII. During his reign he achieved almost next to nothing, yet he is the king that everybody remembers the most. Countless books and films have been made about him. For what reason? It's because men love Henry VIII. He had it all. The power, the money, the women (six of them to be exact). Who in their right mind can cope with six wives? That's six birthdays to remember. Six Valentines. Six sets of in-laws. Six doghouses. The man's a hero.

One story that clearly illustrates why he should be the hero king of man history is the time he travelled to France to meet his keenest rival of the day, King Francis I. The great meeting was designed to strengthen the friendship of the two kings and cement an earlier peace treaty. However, it soon became clear that the French king was gaining the upper hand in negotiations. Now, most normal kings would try and manoeuvre themselves into pole position with diplomacy or other tactical means. Henry said, 'Fuck this. Let's wrestle.' Wrestlemania was born. He lost but the point was made. If only our modern leaders would settle things with a wrestling match, maybe we wouldn't have so many wars.

Just think, the whole Iraq debacle could have been avoided if George W. Bush had challenged Saddam to a smackdown on the front lawn of the White House. The message Henry VIII taught us is clear. Men love to wrestle with each other. With mates or rival kings.

SMOKES AND SPUDS

Now you'd think Henry's daughter Elizabeth I wouldn't have a place in a chapter about man history but you'd be wrong. She was England's ruler for 45 years and again subject of many period dramas, all of them dull. However, her reign is a minefield for man history. England was in a unique position. It now had a hot 25-year-old as queen. We all know men are prepared to do almost anything to impress a woman, but the Elizabethan age was punctuated with constant attempts from the leading men of the realm to outdo each other.

The two most famous men vying for her attention were a pair of sirs. Sir Francis Drake and Sir Walter Raleigh. These days men try and impress girls by popping down to H. Samuel's and buying them a diamanté necklace. Sir Walter really set the bar high when he travelled to the Americas. He named a whole colony after Elizabeth and then brought her back not one but two brand new items. Tobacco and potatoes. The old smoothie. What woman wouldn't fall for a man who brings her smokes *and* spuds?

HOW DO YOU LIKE IT DONE?

Elizabeth's successor was the first Stuart monarch of England, James I, who doesn't really have much to add to the history of men apart from the curious story that he might have invented one of our favourite pieces of meat ever. He was a strange man who spoke with a lisp and dribbled quite a bit. These days he would have worked in IT.

James I was such a fan of good meat that when he was once presented with a really high-quality loin of beef for his dinner, he pulled out his sword and uttered the words, 'I dub thee Sir-loin.' It's interesting to think that without James I, Aberdeen Angus steakhouses may never have existed.

He also reigned during the Gunpowder Plot of 1605 where ex-soldier and Catholic Guy Fawkes attempted to blow up Parliament while the Protestant king was inside it. Although the barrels had been placed many months before in a cellar under the House of Lords, and were ready for igniting, Fawkes was caught when he made the cardinal sin of going back to the unlit fuses. Ironically, this fact is of course celebrated each year by men across the country on Bonfire Night. It's every man's divine right to ignore the shouts of 'NO, DAD, YOU'LL BE BLINDED' and stride over to the firework that's failed to go off, as if we can make it work by igniting it with sheer testosterone. Guy Fawkes was tortured and hung, drawn and quartered but I'd like to think he died for our right to perform this very act.

MEN AND MOTORS

I'll now fast-forward again and channel-hop to the bit of man history that gave us something we love to this very day. Who actually invented the car? There is much speculation about who can lay claim to being the one that gave us the four-wheeled love of our lives.

We do know that in 1769, the very first self-propelled road vehicle was a military tractor invented by French engineer and mechanic Nicolas Joseph Cugnot. He used a steam engine to power his contraption. It was used by the French army to haul artillery at a whopping speed of 2.5 mph. I'm guessing, it being the French army, this was in reverse.

The following year Cugnot built a steam-powered tricycle that carried four passengers. There are few details about whether this was the first ever road trip with the Cugmeister and his entourage going cruising for ladies. Arguing like all men do about who has to sit in the back and who gets the all-important role as wingman up front.

A year later Cugnot drove one of his road vehicles into a stone wall, making him the first person to get into a motor vehicle accident. Were there the high-visibility jacket-wearing wombles putting lane closures all around him? I haven't read his insurance claim but what's the guessing he was distracted by something, say a woman. According to a recent survey, men are more likely than women to get distracted while driving. No shit Sherlock. It even said *killing insects* was a hazardous distraction for men. It's true. We do get very upset about midges on the windscreen. The windscreen is one of the few surfaces a man will try to keep meticulously clean. Work surfaces in the kitchen not so much.

So Frenchie invented the automobile. Or did he? Petrolheads will get very worked up and tell you it was the Germans who were there first. As always in life, the perennial towel on the sun loungers of history. Saying that, Karl Benz did create the first gas-powered vehicles, which are closer to the cars we know today. I'm going to leave it there as I'm beginning to get bored by all the men bickering about cars.

ANOTHER FIRST IN MAN HISTORY

On to some more interesting happenings in our history. Napoleon Bonaparte, the scourge of Europe, invading Italy, Spain, Holland and even Russia. As I said earlier, just being a great figure in history isn't enough to be included in this book – you have to have contributed to man history. Sure, Napoleon ended feudalism in Europe, laid the basis for modern French law and was probably the greatest battlefield commander that ever lived, *but what did he do for men?*

Napoleon, by simply uttering three little words, challenged one of the great injustices that is suffered by men every single day. He was the first person brave enough to say '*Not tonight Josephine*' to his wife. It's fine for a woman to decline sex with her husband, and rightly so, but if a man decides he's not in the mood, a big can of worms is opened.

The woman automatically assumes that they no longer find them attractive and that they're probably having an affair. They also think: I'm better looking than this jerk, he's lucky I'm even giving him a chance. It blows a woman's mind when a man says he just wants a cuddle and does *just want a cuddle*. Without the usual stab in the belly. They don't understand it.

You're a red-blooded man with a penis and you're saying you don't want sex? The man maths just doesn't add up. 'Have penis must use it' is how they think we are. They deduce all that even though it's probably because we've just had a big meal and feel a bit bloated. Suffering from a PMT for men. Post Meal Tiredness. Napoleon was the first man to draw a line in the sand and for that we should get down on our knees and kiss his feet, even though he was French and apparently wore over a litre of cologne a day. Probably to try and hide his smell of Frenchness.

THE TWENTIETH CENTURY

By the turn of the twentieth century, we had become the Chelsea of the day. No one liked us and everybody wanted to beat us at home.

The terrible wars defined these times, but I need to draw attention to something without which we wouldn't be who we are today. Something came along that is possibly the greatest gift man history ever got. No, not fishnet tights.

The television was invented. As the sage Homer Simpson says: 'TV, teacher, mother, secret lover.'

Thanks to John Logie Baird, we now had an excuse not to talk in the house. On 2 October 1925, Baird successfully transmitted the first television picture. It was the head of a ventriloquist's dummy nicknamed 'Stooky Bill'. Shame he had to ruin the moment with a ventriloquist act but he was Scottish and we should be grateful he didn't put the thing in a deep-fat fryer and batter it. He needed another man to help him achieve this remarkable feat and Baird went downstairs and fetched an office worker, 20-year-old William Edward Taynton, to see what a human face would look like.

Taynton became the first person to be televised. I would imagine that when Baird showed this moving image and face, another first was born: 'Is this all that's on?' was said for the first time.

So here's to John Logie Baird, giving men another long-lasting relationship in their lives. Maybe the biggest since being introduced to fire or to the wheel. Neither of those two could give us *Going for Gold* or *Wacky Races* though.

You could sum up the Second World War as a pub car park fight. Just when you thought it was finished, everyone had taken a beating and the bouncers had broken it up, someone makes a snide remark and it all kicks off again.

Luckily for men all over the world, Hitler and the Third Reich were resoundingly kicked into submission. Obviously if he had won it would have been bad for the simple reason that he was a horrible dictator hell bent on world domination and also wanted to wipe out quite a few races on the way. Hitler was also a teetotal vegetarian.

With war off the menu for a bit, men had time to breathe a sigh of relief and push new boundaries and do something other than kill each other. Like get back to the important man business of trying to have sex. One of the big changes after the war was the wide-scale availability of the contraceptive pill. The very idea of consequence-free sex is the holy grail for men. The rhythm method was never perfect for a man: as its name suggests, it's reliant on the very thing men don't have. Rhythm. Men cannot dance.

During the fifties one of the most essential things for life was developed: rock and roll. Sure, rock copied from the blues and so began a lifetime of thievery in rock and roll. One thing's for sure, if Elvis Presley hadn't been invented the world would have been a poorer place. We would never have known about the joys of fried peanut butter sandwiches. Somewhere along the way Kenny Loggins sat down and penned 'Footloose'. History thanks all of rock's Kennys: Loggins and Rogers.

Men now had another way to try and get laid. By forming bands. Singers may bang on about alienation and being disaffected but, come on, no one starts a band so spotty kids can like them. If you couldn't impress the girls at school by getting in the football team the alternative was being in a band. And maybe it's best those two never mix. Music and football are never a pretty combination. Apart from John Barnes's rap on 'World In Motion'.

On 10 April 1951 Steven Seagal was born. Born so that men channel-hopping at one in the morning could find something classy to watch. In most of his great works a simple formula is observed. Steven is a retired US Navy Seal/secret agent/assassin now working as a chef/handyman/IT tech support. Then some bad stuff happens and Steven goes and gets an old bag under his bed that has all of his old killing stuff in and goes back to what he knows best. This book recognises Steven Seagal and will have more on this incredible man later.

By the time Neil Armstrong had stepped down from the lunar landing module on 20 July 1969, America had spent $28 billion and employed just under half a million people in the Apollo programme. Yet they still didn't know if space pirates existed up there, which is what I was looking for through my binoculars every night as a kid. That and really believing about mice drilling for cheese on the moon.

The only useful thing to come out of the Apollo space programme was the invention of Teflon, which means men don't stick their eggs to frying pans any more (well, that much anyway). But it proves that given the chance, men will waste money in the most spectacular way possible.

THE GODFATHER OF PORN

It wasn't all bad, though: the last 50 years have seen men invent some amazing things. As previously mentioned, the microwave oven thanks to Professor Spencer – one of the greatest man inventions. Also consider the internet. Never mind the fact that you can scour the world's greatest works of literature online or get all your weekly shopping without ever leaving the house, the main pull of the internet for men is porn. No more do they have to skulk in the shadows of a newsagent's waiting for a lack of customers at a till. No longer do they have to pull up a creaky floorboard to get out the stash. Now it's all at our fingertips. Tim Berners-Lee is referred to as the 'father of the internet'. He is in fact the godfather of porn.

Technology has moved at an incredible pace. Televisions have got better and bigger and bigger again. Soon your entire living room wall will just be a TV, and you will still be mumbling, 'Should have got a bigger one.'

But not all technological advances have been to the benefit of men. Witness our enslavement by the mobile phone. Fifteen years ago, we could go where we wanted and no one would bother us.

We could head off down the pub for a few misspent hours and no one would ever know. Now we can be tracked down and worse, contacted, EVERYWHERE. Phones are evil. Just look at poor Jack Bauer. If he threw the damn phone away, he could chill out for a day.

We have made some incredible advancements but in the last few years our evolution has reversed at times. I'm not just talking about *Big Brother* contestants. I blame much of this on two things. One: man bags. It was pleasing to see in *The Bourne Ultimatum* that the *Guardian* journalist sporting a man bag was assassinated very early in the movie. Two: low-slung denim. You know what I'm talking about – the fools that wear jeans hanging around their knees, with no belt. If you're 14, fine. Not if you're a man. Martin Freeman, best known as Tim from *The Office* and now a movie star, was on my radio show and made a very fair point on this man wrong. 'Is that the Dunkirk spirit? I don't think so. We couldn't have won the war in baggy denim.'

So we come to the year 2008 in my totally unreliable history of men and the news that men all over the world are talking about... a man is pregnant. That's right. One of us is up the duff. A woman has had something called 'gender realignment' surgery, which I think is what Andrew Lloyd Webber has had on his face. Maybe it's my TV but I'm sure that's a bollock where his head should normally be.

KEY MOMENTS IN MAN HISTORY

Monkeys or mice?

Choose monkey

Find fire. Love it

Egyptians invent booze. Cheers

Greeks give men sport

Caesar gets a comb-over

Two men outdo each other for a woman. With spuds and fags

1769: Car invented. Let's ignore the fact it came from France

A short-arse Frenchie called Napoleon turns down a shag

1925: TV. Pass the remote, please

1945: Germany defeated by port-swigging cigar-chomping Brit

1950s: Rock and roll

1951: Steven Seagal born

1953: A man called Norm invents WD-40

1968: *Columbo* aired for first time

1972: *The Godfather* is released

1975: Charlize Theron is born

1977: Pot Noodles

2001: Sky Plus arrives

IV

MEN AND THEIR MATES

THE LOVE THAT DARE NOT SPEAK ITS NAME

Much has been devoted to our relationships with women, which we will come to in good time. But men's relationships with other men, their buddies, mates and old muckers, are rarely discussed. They are full of unspoken weird rituals, rules and codes. And there are serious repercussions for breaching them.

It's a constant mystery to women what we actually talk about when we get together with our mates. 'Not much' is usually the reply. I sometimes think they feel we are planning a secret man uprising, an escape committee like Steve McQueen and Dickie in *The Great Escape*. The very idea of a man uprising is stupid. There's far too much organising and effort involved for a start. Plus it can't be this Tuesday as the missus has her yoga class and I'm looking after the kids. How's next Monday?

Women think we bond with each other over endless boring sports chats, booze and bottom coughs. What they don't know is that, like them, we also chat about our other halves. Just not with the same level of intimacy or detail. What they also don't realise is that men operate under a series of complex rules and codes. We all know they exist, the unwritten rules, and I have recorded them here for the first time in history.

As we get into relationships and start families, actually getting to see your mates gets harder and harder. Most women immediately fear, distrust and even hate your mates.

They edge them out and restrict your visiting times, or even worse, come with you when you go out with them. She might as well hold your hand or put your balls in her handbag. Your man card* has been revoked.

THE DIARY

Women often utter the phrase, 'That's not in the diary,' when you remind her tomorrow is the night you're hooking up with some old chums. A date you got proper clearance on and did all the relevant paperwork for a while ago. This date probably required days of groundwork (interesting how men often use building phrases to describe relationships – 'groundwork', 'shaky foundations', 'preparation'). Perhaps you tidied some of your

---

*A man card is a card all men are given at birth. It entitles you to act like a man. If you fail to do so, it can be taken away (see The Future of Men).

mess up, said her hair looks nice or removed some of the old takeaway cartons from the fridge.

The simple truth is you will never see the 'diary' in question as it doesn't exist. If it did it would just read: YOU WILL NEVER SEE YOUR FRIENDS AGAIN AS THEY ARE ARSEHOLES AND I HATE THEM.

Maybe women are scared of the bond we have with other men, or scared that whenever we see them we drink too much and are sick over ourselves and on occasion over them. 'You behave differently,' they often say – and they're right. Our mental age is somewhat lowered in the company of other men.

THE PERILS OF WHISPERING

I have also noticed women really don't like that way we whisper among ourselves and then laugh really loudly. If you're ever asked what you were laughing at, always lie. Don't tell them the truth. No matter what they threaten you with.

Last Christmas my refusal to rat out myself and my brother-in-law about what we found so funny got me the stink eye (*see* Men and Women) for a few hours but it's a rap you have to take. No one likes a snitch. It's like Steve McQueen as 'The Cooler King' in *The Great Escape* – you do your time. However, I wasn't allowed any ball games to pass the time.

Between you and me, my brother-in-law and I had discovered that you can instant message each other on a Nintendo DS. (Well, the kids had shown us – we didn't discover it. The boy is the father of the man.) Hey presto, within seconds of finding this out we were sending vulgar messages to each other on them while sitting among relatives.

I'd imagine this happens at those UN meetings. Gordon Brown sending Sarkozy a note saying 'Check out the baba jangers on the babe from Slovenia!' or 'Don't fancy yours much' and nodding at the delegate from Albania.

It transformed the dreaded post-turkey slump into playground fun. My brother-in-law laughed too loudly though. Schoolboy error.

It drew attention to us and the game was up. To this day it's recalled frequently by my wife. I'll take the content of those vulgar messages to my grave. Giggling.

COOKING

I have a friend who is a former Royal Marine Commando, now working as a bodyguard in Afghanistan. A tough guy. Last year, after coming home from a three-month spell away, we went out for drinks. Much later, he was dropped off at home, takeaway Chinese in hand, which he duly ate while his wife was sleeping peacefully upstairs.

Sadly my friend was in a rather confused state (maybe post-traumatic stress disorder, or possibly that extra Stella) and, seeking something to wipe his dirty Chinese sweet and sour hands on, mistook his wife's newly purchased white jacket for a tea towel. In the morning he was awoken by a blood-curdling cry to rival anything he had faced in Afghanistan or Iraq from the mullahs. He had a fear like he had never known before. The immediate discussion of course centred on why whenever he saw his mates he 'needed to get in such a terrible state'.

I remember meeting up with my best mate Phil and returning home slightly the worse for wear. Putting on all the lights in every single room, I then started to cook. Men often like to cook when drunk. I wouldn't be surprised to find out that a drunken guy with the munchies started the Great Fire of London in 1666.

As I was throwing random ingredients into a pan, which I then planned to put between two slices of bread, my lovely wife was upstairs asking in strong Anglo-Saxon terms what was going on and could I just 'get the fuck to bed'. Why don't women just say what they mean?

Feeling a bit sorry for myself, I went and chatted to my dog Digby, who has never used language like that and doesn't judge me. (Dogs don't – that's why they are man's best friend. Cats are judgemental little shits.) And as I was chatting to him, I was struck by how warm and cosy his dog bed was.

The next thing I remember is seeing daylight and my wife towering over me in her dressing gown. Digby was on the other side of the room looking at me as disapprovingly as a little dog (not too little, though – no man should own a small yappy dog) can. Digby wasn't happy.

And it's not just because a few weeks earlier I let my wife get his balls cut off. I picked him up from the vet's and the look in his eyes will stay with me for ever. It wasn't just the pain and disappointment that any man could do this to another man, all be it a man-dog. It was as if he was saying, 'It could be you next.' My wife said getting him done would calm him down, and stop him having sex with any passing dog and urinating on the furniture. My God, I suddenly realised, she wants MY balls removed, she wants my sacred man purse lopped off. To control me; to stop me urinating on the couch (which was an accident).

Think about it. What woman wouldn't want their man neutered? I bet there are back-street man-neutering clinics springing up all over the place right now. An illicit underground network. Run by man-hating women using very rusty implements. With little or no anaesthetic. This explains those too-good-to-be-true men you hear all about from your wife.

'Well, Gill's husband loves going clothes shopping with her and picking out new curtains.'

He's been neutered. You see the neutered men every Saturday limping a few feet behind their women in shopping centres. Thousand-yard stares. I've stumbled on a big global conspiracy here. I bet Bill Clinton has been neutered by now. Just look at the poor fella. That Eliot Spitzer, the disgraced New York governor caught using prostitutes (at least, unlike our feckless MPs, he didn't claim it on his expenses), was probably neutered the moment that public apology was done.

No, the real reason Digby is on my wife's side is that I had slept in his bed that night. A dog bed. That really stinks. The sight that greeted my wife was of a pissed-off-looking dog and my head and shoulders in the dog basket, with the rest of me a tangled heap looking as if I had fallen from a great height. All the lights were still on and for some reason there were spaghetti hoops in my hands.

'Nice seeing your mates again?'

THE SEXY BLACK WIDOW SYNDROME

Women think they have smarter, more emotionally mature relationships than we do with our mates. Bollocks. It runs deeper than a headlock. A bit.

Sure, when guys get together alcohol is often involved and as a consequence so is stupidity. This doesn't help the case for more Mate Time. When women get together, a nice civilised coffee and a Danish is enough. I sometimes envy the simplicity of this. No need for vomiting and hangovers. None of those conversations around midnight about jacking it all in and starting a business together selling monkey butlers door to door.

Don't be fooled, though. Ladies' conversation is rarely civilised. Gossip and bitching. And you know what they discuss when they go to the toilets together? Us. And our winkies. I wonder if other animals do this?

Sexy Black Widow 1: You should have seen the tackle on the one I had last night! Hung like a gnat.

Sexy Black Widow 2: Ha ha ha! Last night's date ended with him crying, saying, 'This doesn't normally happen,' as his web shot off real quick. How I laughed as I ate him...

All Sexy Black Widows together:
Hahahahahahahahahahahahahahahahahahaha!

THE VICIOUSNESS OF WOMEN

I would take my relationship with my mates over women's any day.

I'm serious. A man can break a woman's heart but that is nothing compared to the vicious damage women regularly inflict on each other. Smiling assassins. All nice to their faces but hidden away with another friend/witch and the gloves are off. If *Goodfellas* had been *Goodgirls* the violence would have been far worse. With hair straighteners and nail files.

'You're saying I've put on weight? Put on weight how? How exactly do you find me weighty?'

Men can be cruel to each other but they do it to each other's face. Dignified. Your clothes, hair, beer gut, bald spot, wife, girlfriend, football team, birth place, penis size, girth, salary, sexual orientation, everything. It's all fair game. It's a sign of proper, deep friendship that a mate can safely say 'What the fuck are you wearing?' when you turn up in a brand new shirt you thought you might be mistaken for Brad Pitt in. With a beer gut and bald spot.

Women's friendships are generally more emotionally mature, but they are also more emotionally tedious. Discussions about problems and disputes with friends, feelings about things, can happily carry on for several days without any intake of breath. Is it possible that women can use their handbags as gills?

MEN AND PROBLEMS

This annoys us men as we are hardwired, when confronted with a problem, to solve it. To a man a problem shared is like being handed a bomb that needs to be defused as quickly as possible. To us it all comes down to which wire to cut. The red one or the blue one?

This is opposed to just talking about it A LOT. It's man DNA: men are problem solvers. Not always very good solvers, but solvers all the same. Last year my wife told me to get Ruby our eldest daughter's hair cut but not to spend too much money on it. Quick as a flash I had processed this order and come up with a smart solution: I'd cut it myself.

With no formal training I cut my daughter's hair. Can you guess what happened next? Even Ruby looked confused as I set about her fringe. With paper scissors. The fringe that my wife had proudly been cultivating for the last six months. Problem

solvers. My wife came back home and let's just say hilarity did
not ensue.

MALE PROBLEM SOLVERS EXTRAORDINAIRE

Back to men and their mates. Men in the
company of other men are
capable of great feats of ingenuity
– like Stonehenge, say. Actually,
that might not be the best
example. Relocating some big
rocks. Beer must have been
involved.

Men do like to carry interesting objects home from the pub. It's
one of the rare times we enjoy shopping. Or man's other great
motivator:

> 'You heard why we're humping these great big things?'

> 'For gullible hippies and dumb American tourists?'

> 'Nope, some idiot wants to get in some girl's knickers.'

Men with other men are also capable of great feats of stupidity.

The Darwin Awards celebrate those who 'improve our gene pool
by removing themselves from it'. They record for us and future
generations some darkly funny accidental deaths, mostly featuring
men, with other men, and alcohol.

Tony Roberts, 25, lost his right eye having been shot through the skull by a hunting arrow during an initiation into a men's rafting club, Mountain Men Anonymous (probably known now as Stupid Mountain Men Anonymous) in Grants Pass, Oregon.

What a deadly combination, men with hunting gear and alcohol. (Might make a good episode of *Holby City*, though). What happened here, I understand, is a good friend of Tony's tried to shoot a beer can off his head. It would have had to have been a close friend, of course – couldn't let a complete stranger do something as intimate as shooting at you with large arrows.

Many clubs and societies have some kind of entrance exam, and Mountain Men Anonymous's test was having someone shoot an arrow at your head while pissed. It's natural selection: they only want the very finest minds entering. With or without bits of metal protruding from them.

I bet his first words after being released from hospital were, 'Did I pass? Am I in Mountain Men Anonymous?'

That is nothing compared to what I think is the definitive story of the danger present when two lethal substances come into contact:

$$\text{Man} + \text{Man} \times \text{Beer} = \text{Idea}$$

Let us examine the tale of Sal Hawkins and John Pernicky, two huge Metallica fans. They showed up to where the band was playing in Washington but they had no tickets so sat in the car park drinking beer, thinking the situation over. Suddenly a genius idea occurred. Inspiration. The mother of invention is necessity, they say, but swap necessity for beer and they had something.

A plan was hatched after they noticed that the perimeter fence was only nine foot high and no possible deterrent to two sharp men like themselves. Problem solvers like all men. They then decided to pull their pick-up truck (we could have guessed they drove one of them) over to the fence.

The plan was that John, the heavier of the two, was to hop over and then help his buddy over. Simple. What could possibly go wrong?

Sadly, the fence had a 30-foot drop on the other side. So when John launched himself over like some nubile gymnast from the former Eastern Bloc, he found himself crashing through a big tree, a large branch stopping his descent by snagging his shorts. Dangling from the tree with one arm broken, John saw some bushes beneath him and, being one of nature's problem solvers, thought he would simply cut away his shorts with his penknife and then drop to the bushes below him. (Must have seen MacGyver or The A Team do something pretty similar.)

Once free of his shorts, John fell down into what he now realised were holly bushes. They scratched him everywhere and, without the protection of his shorts, one branch entered his rectal cavity. It gets worse. The penknife dropped too and when he landed it went three inches into his thigh. Sal saw his buddy in all this pain and sprung into man action. A problem-solving man in action is a sight to see. He threw his fallen comrade a rope, but as John was a big fella, Sal couldn't pull him too well. Not to worry, try something else, as you never let a mate down. Especially if the mate is partially naked with a branch up his arse. So he attached the rope to the pick-up truck.

This is where it goes really bad.

Sal, in his drunken state, puts the thing in reverse and crashes through the fence, landing flat on top of his mate. Killing him. Sal is thrown from the vehicle and also dies.

The police arrive. Picture the scene that awaits them. Even *CSI*'s Gil Grissom would have been confused by this one. A pick-up truck with its driver thrown 100 feet away, and then under the truck a semi-naked man, covered in scratches with a holly branch up his rectum, a knife in his leg, and his shorts in a tree.

Here's to you, John and Sal, two fine minds and men taken from us. Some sort of commemorative statue would be a fitting tribute to these real men of genius. Bronze, I'm thinking, depicting the final sad scene. Branch up bum, truck on top, the whole deal. Men from all over the world could come and pay tribute. Should be placed on the Washington town hall steps. A Man Lourdes. Kids could be taken there to warn them about the dangers of alcohol and, more importantly, being a man.

I feel you also need to know and respect a Polish farmer called Krystof Azninski who in 1995... er... there's no easy way to put this, cut his own head off.

Guess what? He had been drinking with male friends. Apparently one of the gathered geniuses (or is the plural genii?) casually suggested they strip naked and play some 'men's games'.

What was I saying about men together? It's all fun and games until someone loses a head.

And we wonder why women think we behave like dicks when we are together. Never seen the *Sex and the City* girls behaving like that? Might watch it if they did.

Back to the naked men and the 'men's games'. They start off with a good old round of hitting each other over the head with frozen turnips. No, really. Frozen turnips. Then, as is usually the case, one of the men ups the stakes by getting a chainsaw and CUTTING HIS OWN FOOT OFF.

Now, we weren't there but you don't have to wonder at what happened next. Put men together and some form of one-upmanship will occur. It can be the swapping of increasingly tall stories with the final ones being 100 per cent bona fide bullshit; sometimes it's shots being ordered to 'get the party started'; sometimes it's the removal of limbs. Did any of the men say, 'OK, that's enough now – we've all had a few drinks and smashed frozen turnips over our heads, pretty soon someone's gonna get hurt'?

No, they didn't.

Azninski shouted 'WATCH THIS!' as he swung the chainsaw at his head, taking it off. His head. Off.

'It's funny, when he was young he put on his sister's underwear. But he died like a man,' one of those fine men friends said. I think I speak for all of us when I say who would want a more fitting way to be remembered by friends and family?

THE WORLD'S DUMBEST MAN SHOW

I wonder whether there should be a TV show called *The World's Dumbest Man*. Think about the enjoyment we still have watching *The World's Strongest Man*: 'Sven the big guy from Iceland is really coping well with the 2CV he's carrying this year – awesome stuff.' *The World's Dumbest Man* is the next generation. Teams of men from around the world would enter with their mates, as we all know that men are spurred on to even greater feats of stupidity when with their mates. Britain could do well at this. Alcohol would feature in most events.

THE WORLD'S DUMBEST MAN SHOW EVENTS

Chair Sitting. Last man still just sitting in an armchair wins. This could take some time; months even.

Man Tears Challenge. Can any man sit through an episode of *Extreme Makeover* or Rolf's *Animal Hospital* (featuring dogs passing away) or *The Champ* without crying?

Synchronised Toenail Clipping. (I once saw a man doing this on a train. I was both horrified and impressed.)

Mattress Endurance Challenge. Teams have one mattress to transport as far as they can using a small family car. It can only go on the roof and no ropes are allowed. It's the classic man driving with one arm on the mattress.

These man games would include Freestyle Bullshitting, where male entrants must talk about anything that has or has not happened to them and then lie about it. As we do. Men are born bullshitters; it is in our DNA. That's why most car salesmen are men. Pat Butcher included.

Even smart, educated, brave men let their man DNA get the better of them. It would appear that our entire sense of logic and reasoning is drastically altered when in proximity to other men. Man molecules affect and change other man molecules, causing a Man Big Bang.

Imagine you work at the international space station doing important astronaut space work. You wake up in your astronaut bed one day and think:

a) I should go and collect some rock samples so mankind can learn about the life forms up here

b) I should see how far I can hit a golf ball into space with a gold-plated six iron and film it

b) is what Expedition 14 commanders Michael Lopez-Alegria and Mikhail Tyurin went for. Boys together. In space. Hitting golf balls. Doing important work.

In case you're wondering about the gravity during the shot, Lopez-Alegria held Tyurin's feet, which were affixed to a ladder. Tyurin carried three golf balls, but only had time to hit one of them before ground flight controllers instructed the spacewalkers to proceed to their other tasks.

I love that. He held his feet. Don't tell me we fear intimacy. Here we have two grown men, astronauts who have trained for years, for crying out loud, who agree that one will hold the other's space boots. Playing Intergalactic Golf. It's a real shame that the boring ground controllers made them 'proceed to their other tasks' rather than hit some more balls. What could possibly be more important than this task? There is, however, a sad end note to this.

The golf ball did not travel in the full retrograde direction, away from the space station, as intended. Instead, Tyurin shanked the ball.

So we go from 'One small step for man, one giant leap for mankind' to 'Told you you should've used the five iron, dickhead.' Even in space men together will do something stupid. It's the collision of man molecules. You ask Professor Hawking. I bet the Hawkman, when he gets together with his mates, arses about like any man.

SO HOW DO OUR RELATIONSHIPS COMPARE TO WOMEN'S?

Time after time, research findings conclude that women have deeper and longer-lasting relationships than men. And have more friends. We apparently have superficial friendships that consist of mumbling into cold beers and never saying anything of any emotional worth.

Scared stiff of saying what we really feel, we keep it all in. Then have heart attacks and explode, leaving all our mates going, 'He never said anything was up.'

So women say we don't communicate enough. However, it is my serious contention after years of intensive research that men use a far higher dimension to communicate with each other. It's a previously undiscovered man bandwidth we operate on. The Manwidth. I will be taking my incredible findings of its existence around the world.

Just go into any pub and you will see men communicating by silence and osmosis. This is how many of our dads told us the facts of life. Silence and nods and 'ask your mum'. A chat most dads dreaded and now with easy internet access happily don't need to.

That said, men can easily get into very heated discussions about certain things in the pub, sometimes leading to fights. We will learn later that this tradition goes back thousands of years. I once had to separate two mates who started fighting after an intense chat about star signs. No, really. It was after the line 'All Aquarians are c**ts' that fists started to fly. If only Russell Grant had been on hand to help settle the whole 'Aquarian C**ts' debate.

A study conducted by Manchester University found that almost half of the women asked kept in touch with their best mate every day. Every day! For me to call a best mate there has to be a reason to call, something specific, otherwise it's just plain wrong. For men it was 36 per cent. It should have been lower. Who the hell wants a mate that bothers you all the time? We hate being hassled. My wife is constantly texting her network of mates, often within three seconds of just speaking to them for two hours.

Only a woman can see a friend for the entire day and still find something to talk to them about on the phone later that night. No sane man would do this with his mate. Women seem to fear being dumped and so try really hard to be the best possible friend. They put much more effort into the deal.

Effort in our relationships is getting your round in. Women buy gifts for

each other. We don't do that. I may have bought them a drink to mark the day but... a gift?

Many women have now upgraded from texting to Facebook. The huge popularity of these social networking sites have passed me by. No real man has any business on them unless they're a pervert or stalker. Women like them because they are nosy and want to see if the prettiest girl in the school is now hideously obese and working on the till at Wilkinson's. That's when they're not looking up an ex-boyfriend from Class 4b.

Men just want to see if the popular football captain who never picked you has gone bald or the weird kid whose parents never let him watch TV has killed anyone. Is it really for tracking down old friends or is it for seeing (and hoping) that other people's lives have turned out worse than ours? If I wanted to be in contact with you, I would be. If we lost touch, it's for a reason.

I think a far better website for men would be ToolsReunited or whencanihaveitback.com. One of the worst man crimes is borrowing something from a mate, be it a tool like a jigsaw or drill bit or a DVD box set of 24, and then not giving it back. It's worse than trying to nail his wife. (*See* The Men Commandments.)

Man invented the web and what a surprise it is that this exciting new world of possibilities fast became a super-quick way to see women's naughty bits. When I was a kid I was fascinated and excited by Asimov's pictures of the bold new future that awaited us. Cities in the air, jetpacks transporting us. What he failed to

---

QUICK TOP FIVE BEST LOCAL BOOZERS IN TV SHOWS, IN NO PARTICULAR ORDER:

The Winchester, *Minder*: 'Hullo, Arthur'

The Nags Head, *Only Fools and Horses*: Deadly food, Mike the barman

Cheers Bar, *Cheers*: The ideal, never ever be like that, but still a great bar

Moe's Bar, *The Simpsons*: Remember when Homer asked for Candy Beer he thought he'd seen advertised on TV that had skittles floating in the top?

Bada Bing, *Sopranos*: How are you meant to run a Mafia empire with topless girls in the office?

see was the internet and the jetpack inventors, derailed from their pioneering work, bent double over their PCs, jerking off.

Thank God the internet and its corrupting influence on some men's minds wasn't around when they were building the pyramids. They would be half-finished like most projects men undertake. Wembley Stadium might have been finished earlier had a few of the workers' wives gone down daily to check on progress.

Social networking for men used to be down the local pub but the local pub is now dying out. Pubs are now frequented by thugs and loudmouths or they're part of a hideous chain.

THE JOY OF TEXT

I mentioned earlier that women are constantly texting each other. To men, texting is more a tool for abuse: 'u ok fat b*stard?'

Oh, and for passing on poor-taste jokes after a national disaster. Lorry drivers used to transport jokes around the country; now it's done by SMS. That's progress. It's also a simpler way for men to communicate than a phone call that could go on for over a minute.

Men fear the phone. We view it as highly suspicious. I refuse to answer the landline at home.

'Can you get that?'

'No, it'll be for you.'

Even if a man does pick up the landline, he will forget to take any message because his mind just freezes.

'Some mate of yours called.'

'Who?'

'No idea.'

'You mean you didn't take a name or number?'

'She'll call back if it's important.'

A guy could go 30 years without seeing his mate, and still only speak for no more than a few minutes on the phone. I bet when Dr Livingstone and Stanley finally met up after being lost along the Nile, the reunion was something like this:

'Dr Livingstone, I presume...'

'Yup.'

'Where the fuck have you been?'

'Don't ask, got lost.'

'See you soon.'

'Give us a call.'

'Bye.'

WHAT WE TALK ABOUT

A timer goes off the moment any man starts a phone call. He may not be aware of it but it does. Sadly many younger men have had this device eradicated by the world we live in. Air fresheners and pot pourri have polluted and feminised our man minds. You see young guys on trains and buses talking moronically about nothing. Not last night's game or TV, just noise. How did this happen?

Forget the panic about our man juice and declining fertility rates, it's the rise in phone call duration that needs addressing. We need a parliamentary think tank. Or maybe all mobiles should be fitted with a device that automatically ends any call that goes on over two minutes.

I remember when my best mate Phil proposed and texted me to say his girlfriend had just said yes. My wife was really surprised at this. So was I. We were meeting up in two weeks' time – did it really need the text? She pestered me to call him. I did and we spoke for a few minutes and then afterwards I was asked what he said about the big proposal. Nothing. It didn't come up. Why not? No need. He already said she said yes.

When I meet up with my mates, which these days is every couple of decades, we pick up from where we left off. We don't bore each other with the minute detail of our love lives. Even if one of us announced he had a rare tropical illness and had just days to live, there would be an awkward silence. Someone would then know exactly what to do next. 'Who fancies another pint?' Some may even have wondered what the hell he was playing at, putting everyone on a downer like that. Then the natural order would return. Back to man small talk, which as we all know is:

- Swapping stories

- Bad jokes

- Best trivia

- General bullshitting

- Exaggerating stories by at least 77.7 per cent

- Nostalgia

- Sport

- Really Important Debates like would you suck another man's penis for a million pounds?

If you ever get stuck for something to say and football has been done or one of you isn't a fan then just try asking something like this: 'If you were a time traveller, would you rather travel through time in the USS *Enterprise* from *Star Trek* or in the Tardis?'

I wasted several hours of my poor listeners' lives on this one, time they will never get back, and we got calls and emails from all over the world for days. For the record, I'm saying the *Enterprise*. Why? you ask.

Shatner had a great chair, the Captain's Chair. He also had a huge widescreen TV right in front of it. Great uniform too. Plus the teleporter. *Enterprise* rocked.

Dr Who stands in that shabby phone box. We all know phone boxes stink of wee. He does have a pretty cool sonic screwdriver but he doesn't have a good chair, or a widescreen TV.

After giving my choice on the show, David Tennant called in to take issue. He even called the great Captain James T. Kirk a 'war mongerer and Bush-loving imperialist'.

Men bond through bullshitting, bravado, trivia and a shared common experience of how women behave in ever more confusing ways – confusing to us, anyway. It's our currency. These are the cornerstones of any male friendship.

Our friendships are also very loyal. Some men have trouble being loyal to their partner but to his best mate, underpants or football team, well, those things are for life. Pant loyalty will be discussed in proper detail later in this book. Don't worry.

SO WHAT DO WOMEN TALK ABOUT?

So what do women and their friends bond through? My guess would be:

- How often they are forced to have sex with their partner. Broken down by week/month/year/decade/millennia

- Group discussion of the dreams they had last night. In detail

- The latest miracle fad diet of the week that will shift inches off your arse

- Round of general man-bashing about how very useless we are around the house, etc, etc

- A final bout of penis size comparison

My findings on this are based on several eavesdropping sessions on my wife and her circle of friends. Once my jaw hit the deck as one of them, I kid you not, said she could actually remember being one year old. Now, did anyone say to her 'Fuck off' as would have been the case in any group of men if someone had said that? No, they didn't. There were just echoes of 'Woooooooow'. Then they all tried really hard to recall their earliest memories. I fell asleep.

TV shows like *Sex and the City* show women's relationships as being much more fun than men's. This programme makes me want to cry. You know why? Because I have a pair of testicles. Men who say they like it are either gay or lying to try and appear all metrosexual when they just want to jump you.

Maybe if I'm honest my feelings for *Sex and the City* are because no man wants to be watching TV with his other half and see her laughing at penis length jokes.

NOTHING BELOW THE BELT

Maybe we need a *Sex and the City* for men. Working on the same formula, it would feature blokes chatting about their other half's breasts and blow job technique. Although the chats about sex stuff in my man version would be pretty dull as we don't really do that. Between men there is an unsaid rule of Nothing Below the Belt, Queensberry rules all round. To discuss such things would mean subconsciously thinking about your mate's penis.

Another man's penis, be he friend or foe, is not something we like dwelling on. Men don't even like seeing other men naked in movies. This isn't some kind of latent homophobia, however. Men love their own bits – it's a gift we are given at birth. Sadly not all men are equal here. Women who think their breasts are inadequate can use padded bras. Do we need padded condoms?

AT THE SHOPS

Women are happy to have fun together going shopping all day. They do it on *Sex and the City* and *Desperate Housewives*. Ever seen James Bond or Jason Bourne doing the sales at Bluewater? Shopping to men is done in the SAS model: 'Get in, get it, and get out.' I don't know if it's the fluorescent lighting but I honestly feel a bit sick after an hour's clothes shopping.

When men go shopping together they don't touch the clothes as much as women do. Women have to knead clothes before they would even consider trying them on. Men just stare at them for a bit. The man with you is not expected to wait outside the dressing room to give their thoughts. If a man pops into the changing room, his mate will just drift off only to reappear later, saying, 'You get it?'

Changing rooms do scare us a bit. There is a tension in there. When we use them and pull back the curtain to find a mirror we almost jump back in fright if confronted by the sight of another man using the mirror, mumbling, 'Oh, sorry,' several times. Why is that?

The thought of sharing, even accidentally, a mirror with another man is too much. We would be looking at each other. What if we liked what we saw?

Looks become touches, become cuddles... NO! MAKE IT STOP! The sexual tension. Is that how those two cowboys in *Brokeback* first started their relationship?

Changing rooms are not man friendly. The enforced intimacy is not good for us. Just hearing another strange man undoing his trousers and taking his shirt off makes us feel funny. The curtain needs to be a steel two-foot-thick door, the flimsy rooms cells with reinforced walls. The steel doors, like prisons, should only slam open when there is no man out in 'no-man's-land' where the shared mirror is.

When our wives and girlfriends are with us we get irritated if they casually fling the curtain back to see how we are getting on with those jeans. 'Close the curtain! What are you doing in here?'

While I'm on the subject, the man chairs we get outside ladies' changing rooms are wholly inadequate. There is usually only one chair afforded to us per 17 women's changing cubicles.

One man sits in it while others look on, exchanging knowing 'changing-room nightmare' looks. There need to be lazy-boy recliners, or a nice ball pit like kids have at the Wacky Warehouse. Or dodgems for us to play on.

The whole relationship between men is best seen on TV shows like *Top Gear* with Clarkson, May and Hammond. The show when Richard Hammond returned after becoming the new Princess Diana was really emotional for us millions watching. Clarkson just said, 'You're not a bit mental, are you?' But we all knew what he really felt. We just knew.

Sure, we may not say much to each other sometimes but that's the thing about our relationships. We are comfortable with the silences. A nod towards the bar for another drink is all that's needed.

TRUE FRIENDS

True friends are there when we need, not want, them.
I remember many years ago being dumped and suddenly living in London knowing no one. I was dying on my arse doing open-mike stand-up comedy spots in dodgy pubs and working in a call centre during the day. These were not the best of times. Then I made a friend called Justin, who took the piss out of me and my desperate situation. After one drunk-dial phone call to my ex, ending with me shouting some swear words, he calmly just said, 'That seemed to go well.' It was just what I needed. Needless to say we have since lost touch and no, I'm not going on Friends Reunited to track him down.

In the brilliant film *Stand by Me*, the last line always makes me want to start the man tears: 'I never had any friends later on like the ones I had when I was twelve. Jesus, does anybody?'

I'm not crying, it's just some dirt in my eye.

V

MEN AND WOMEN

We know we are very different from them and that they are different from us. But I don't think we are from different planets. I think we are from different galaxies.

Scientists have recently discovered that there are 78 genetic differences between men and women. For the first time in history I have uncovered and detailed all of them. This work is based on extensive field studies, undercover work and making lots of mistakes. I am lucky enough to have my lovely wife on hand to help not only point them out but also help me learn from them. Just as she has done with our dog, who is now successfully house-trained. I, apparently, have some way to go...

1. THE PRETENDING TO BE SORRY GENE IN MEN

Right now you can bet somewhere in the world at least 17,872 men are saying how very sorry they are to a woman. What they are actually sorry for they have no real idea. But, being smart men, they are certainly very sorry about it.

There is an art to saying you're sorry. I call it the Rolf. You need to imagine you are Rolf Harris, but not Rolf doing *Cartoon Club*. Rolf doing *Animal Hospital*. Imagine that you, as Rolf, have to tell someone that their poor old dog never made it through surgery. You would do it well, wouldn't you? With a quiet intensity showing you really understood their pain.

Find your inner Rolf when saying you're sorry, even if you have no idea what you are sorry about. Think dead dog.

2. THE REPLACEMENT GENE IN WOMEN

The gene that recognises that when a loo roll has no more paper on it, this signifies it's time to replace it.

This gene is absent in men. Men will use the very last piece of paper on a loo roll and look down at the bare cardboard cylinder and simply think, hope that gets replaced soon, in the same way a dog looks at his empty bowl.

Men have a genetic anomaly which means they simply sit on the toilet and, not possessing the replacement gene, just shout for someone to come along who does have this gene and do it for them. They yell 'Honey, we're out of loo roll!' in a mixture of anger and surprise. Similar to when we were young boys, going, 'Mum, I've finished!'

The replacement gene in women extends to almost everything in the house that is mysteriously replenished. Washing-up liquid, fabric softener, and those hideous man-musk-hating plug-in air fresheners. Men believe that the Borrowers living in the skirting boards replace all this stuff during the night.

3. THE DIARY GENE IN WOMEN

She who controls the diary, controls.

This is the holy grail for women. The diary. Any time you want some buddy time, it will be referred to the central mother lode diary. Any time you remind them that you're out tomorrow night as previously okayed in accordance with the good book will be flatly denied with the much dreaded phrase:

'That's not in the diary.'

'Yeah but we spoke about it ages ago.'

'Well, it's not in so it's not happening.'

Getting your hands on this beast is like Indiana Jones in the Temple of Doom. Your life is at risk from venom-tipped spikes and a large boulder rolling out of the airing cupboard (they have a gene for those things too, airing cupboards and the running of them).

You might notice that anything you need to go in the diary is put in with a pencil. It's easier to erase, the moment you're out of sight. Her stuff is in ink. Yours pencil. You are never invited or allowed to write in the diary. It's usually brightly coloured to deter you.

Every time I ask a friend if they fancy meeting up they will always mumble, 'I'll have to check with the diary.' I say the same when I'm being asked out to play. A little bit of a man dies when this happens. How often do you find yourself asking on a Thursday, 'What's happening this weekend?'

'We're getting married?'

'Oh, OK.'

Diaries are a form of mind control for men.

4. THE LIST GENE IN WOMEN

The list gene. Women love making a list. So did the Nazis. I'm not making any kind of connection, I'm just saying.

We will be encouraged to take part in the list system. Women can become list fundamentalists and resistance is futile. I will be made, that's right, made, to write a shopping list. It will be checked by my wife before I set off to a supermarket. This has to happen for a very good reason.

When I go with a list I will often return in a hire van full of food that will never be eaten. Meringue mix. Make your own pizza kits. Rare cheeses that are already out of date.

This happens because my man genes kick in. I look at the list once and then never again, thinking my giant man brain has memorised it like I'm on an SAS mission behind enemy lines and cannot be caught with a list detailing my covert operation. When I get back my wife will ask where the bread, milk, eggs and butter are. All I can say is, 'I GOT SOME ECLAIRS! Four for the price of three! Can you believe that?'

5. THE WARDROBE BLINDNESS GENE IN WOMEN

A debilitating genetic illness where the sufferer (a woman) can look at a wardrobe that to a man's eyes is CRAMMED with clothes and proclaim 'I'VE GOT NOTHING TO WEAR!'

You helpfully point out the many, many items clearly visible to your eyes and Google Earth. This is never a good idea. No woman in history has ever at this point just said, 'You know what? You're right. I'm being silly.' Never happens. Just agree and get your credit card out.

Once I went too far and mistook this wardrobe myopia as an opportunity for humour. I enthusiastically agreed and then grabbed a load of these 'useless clothes', took them downstairs and dumped them in the bin, thinking this may be the funniest gag ever. Here's something I can pass on to you. To save your life.

NEVER JOKE WITH A WOMAN ABOUT CLOTHES. YOU WILL REGRET IT ALMOST IMMEDIATELY.

Same with policemen. They don't like jokes by us either. So don't joke around with women about clothes or policemen. Either could get you maced.

6. THE HANDBAG GENE IN WOMEN

Only women enjoy a handbag. I don't even like it when my wife asks me to hold hers. I resist with every man molecule in my body. It feels wrong. That's why man bags are so wrong and yet another example of men being feminised. Man bags are the bisexuals of the bag world.

I hate even going inside a handbag. If my wife asks me to get her purse from her handbag, my face contorts as if she's asked me to put my hand in some dog shit. Man hands are not welcome in there. I'm scared my hand is going to get trapped in it and like a Venus Fly Trap I'll be slowly dragged in and my genitals removed.

Proof that the handbag gene exists only in women is evident when a man tries to buy one as a present. You must get the female shop assistant to help you. Buy one alone and you are not handing your wife a handbag, you're giving her a receipt.

Once they start emptying the thing it's like when Jaws was cut open. All kinds of crap is in there and they are always stocked with a never-ending supply of tissues. And stamps. And two Polo mints.

Men's pockets are our handbags.

7. THE 'WHAT'S HE BEEN IN?' GENE IN WOMEN

It's impossible to watch anything without my wife commentating over it. The classic is the 'What's he been in?', as she goes through various TV shows, agreeing and then disagreeing with herself. It would be a good idea for pop-ups to appear on screen with each actor's name and CV.

Other top five commentary topics include:

- 'He/she is dead.' Often they are annoyingly right.

- 'What did they just say?' You are expected to be like Sky+ and offer instant replays of any given scene.

- 'That doesn't even make sense.' Women's sense of logic and reasoning is far stronger than men's. That's why more boys than girls watched The A Team and none of us had any problem with them being locked in a small shed then building a cabbage gun to take on Uzi-toting mercenaries.

- 'As if that would happen in real life.' Sister comment to the above.

- 'Bet he did it.' Yeah, thanks, Sherlock, no point in watching it now.

8. THE BILL-SPLITTING GENE IN WOMEN

Four men have something to eat together. The bill arrives. It's split into four. Because there's four of them.

Four women have something to eat together. Then over the next 17 minutes they carry out complex PhD-level maths because Jody didn't have the starter or a white wine spritzer and Mandy just had the salad so she just wants to pay for that and that alone. And Claire didn't have any drinks so can you work out her share of JUST THE FOOD AS I ONLY HAD TAP WATER.

If Jesus had invited women instead of his disciples to the last supper they still would have insisted the big guy pay 23.87654999795 per cent of the bill despite the fact he turned the water into wine.

9. THE QUICKSAND QUESTION GENE IN WOMEN

'Do these jeans make my bum look big?'

'Do you like this top?'

'What about these shoes/skirt/whatever?'

If you are asked any of these questions, just give in and accept defeat. You can't answer them because THERE IS NO RIGHT ANSWER. You are in the feared quicksand question zone and if you start to panic too much and flap around you get dragged in deeper. This powerful and alluring female gene has claimed many great men.

If you try and answer too quickly, you are 'just trying to rush me out the door'. Too slowly: 'Sorry, am I boring you?' It's better to just jump out of the window. Though then you run the risk of being called 'overdramatic'.

We all dread being asked the quicksand question and know that every nuance of what we say can and will be used as evidence against us. You are not simply being asked a question. You are being cross-examined. It's a lamb to the slaughter. You are going into a shredder. I'm running out of metaphors here.

If a woman is asking a man's opinion on clothes, it's a loaded question. They are in a bad funk about how they look and feel and somebody needs to feel the force of that. YOU.. You try to console them and you get rebuked with, 'Oh, you would say that – you just want to get some later tonight.' That's probably true.

It's different for a man, though. As we don't have the quicksand question gene, a man rarely asks if a pair of jeans make his arse look big. Men always think they have a great body even when all the physical evidence screams the opposite. Just look at what happens when the weather gets nice and guys start showing too much flesh. Nasty. Some of us need burkhas. Like Andrew Lloyd Webber.

Women will confide in their mates about how they hate their bodies and would love to lose a few pounds. This does not happen so much with men. They will say they want to get fit, which means lose weight. They focus more on the beer gut than arse. Friends will helpfully point out any weight gain. My best friend Phil put some pounds on while his wife was pregnant. I noticed this when he came round once and, not wanting to hurt his feelings, called him 'Fat Phil' for the entire day. His wife said he was very quiet on the journey home. The next day he went to his garage and dusted off his unused (in quite some time) rowing machine. He got on it and broke it. No lie. The little onboard computer kept flashing 'No Coach Parties'. (I'd like to thank the late Les Dawson for that gag.)

You want to flatter any man? Just say 'Do you work out?' and he will be putty in your hands. Even if the fat fuck has never been near a gym in his life he will tell you all about how 'naturally' fit he is and how he was asked to train for the Olympics by a talent scout who spotted him doing bombs in the local swimming pool – but turned it down wanting to pursue a career in IT and chronic masturbation.

10. THE HIDDEN STORAGE GENE IN WOMEN

Women like to have things hidden away in cupboards. Not so for men. I want all my CDs and DVDs on display like war medals. I don't want someone, another man, coming round and thinking I don't own a copy of The Godfather or Arthur on videotape and DVD.

My wife is constantly trying to get them hidden away in those man-hating hidden storage units. Ideally we'd be in those units too. A discreet push and the unit would gently glide open to let us out to deal with the bins.

A sub-genus of the hidden storage gene in women is the next one:

11. THE THROWING THINGS OUT GENE IN WOMEN

Many times I come home and it's like I've been burgled. My stuff, important memorabilia like my signed Evil Knievel picture, has gone. It's either been thrown out or put somewhere like the attic where men's stuff goes to die. No questions about if I still need it. Nope, just thrown out. I would never do this. My life would be in serious danger. It's women performing ethnic cleansing. Nothing is safe. Even your leftover takeaway cartons in the fridge from the other month are gone.

I had to iron a shirt the other week and asked my sweetheart where the ironing board was. Due to some man genetics we will come to shortly, I looked around the space within twelve inches of my body for the ironing board before asking where it was. She'd thrown it out. Why? Because it hadn't been used in a few weeks. In that case, I said, we'd better throw out her vagina too.

This was a mistake. I thought she'd be impressed with my Oscar Wilde-like wit. Even my trusty dog Digby winced when I said it. I went and ordered a new one online, thinking the next day my point would be made upon its arrival. Victory to me! Sadly the impact was somewhat lost when three ironing boards arrived. Did I say I'd had a few glasses of a nice red wine before ordering online? Well, I had, and my big moment disappeared from view with the arrival of three ironing boards. The dog winced again. The only person not slightly intrigued as to why someone would possibly want three ironing boards was the person delivering them. Who was a man. We never question.

This throwing things out gene can suddenly get activated with no prior warning. Once I came back and all my vinyl records had been taken to the Cancer Research shop. I got into my car and drove straight there to reclaim them but lost my nerve as I walked in and started thinking that the cure for cancer might actually be aided from the proceeds of my limited edition seven-inch copy of Nik Kershaw's 'Wide Boy'. I drove home, resolving to make myself a nice cheese and bacon sandwich to ease the pain of never seeing George Michael's cheery face on the cover of 'Last Christmas' again. That was until I saw that the bacon and cheese had been victims of the cleansing programme too. Though not donated to the Cancer Research shop. They went to Oxfam.

12. THE THERMOSTAT GENE IN WOMEN

Women are always cold. Around the home. In bed. Constantly fiddling with the thermostat, wearing nine layers, including your favourite jumper, which they love ruining by putting their legs through the arms.

Men don't have this freezing cold gene – you see guys wandering around perfectly happy in just a T-shirt in the middle of winter. With a pair of flip-flops on.

Women like to place their icy-cold feet on us in bed. They see us men as portable heaters. That smell a bit.

13. THE BITCH GENE IN WOMEN

Man alive, is this gene strong and prevalent in women! You watch any boardroom scenes in The Apprentice. It's like nature in action. All that's missing is a hushed commentary from David Attenborough.

The female's face flushes a deeper shade of red. She then raises her voices and screams, 'I AM TALKING, WILL YOU PLEASE –' to which another woman will shout, 'I AM TALKING... YOU ARE DISRUPTIVE AND TOLD ME... I AM TALKING... THAT DIANE HAS A FAT TUMMY AND LOOKS LIKE A MUFFIN WITH IT SPILLING OVER HER PANTS.'

Women love to bitch about enemies and friends and the two seem to blur into one. Frenemies. Men are rubbish at it. We lack the killer touch and don't enjoy it as much as women do. The simple truth is women enjoy filleting and gutting their friends and rivals. The mere mention of another woman's name will get this gene fired up.

14. THE NANA KNICKERS GENE IN WOMEN

Women moan when we buy them skimpy lingerie, but if we didn't they would just use the passion killer nana knickers they have hidden away until after the ink on the marriage certificate has dried.

These are flame retardant and can in case of an emergency be used as a makeshift parachute. They can also stop an erection dead at 50 paces, which is exactly what they are designed for.

15. THE CURTAIN GENE IN MEN

No man has anything to say about curtains. He has a gene that prevents this. Unless his name is Laurence.

16. THE TALKING GENE IN WOMEN

Women are genetically programmed to love talking. A man needs to be given warning that a conversation is needed. So he has time to think about the talking that may be needed, or time to plan his escape.

The phrases 'We need to have a chat later' or 'We need to talk, not now, later' can turn a happy man into a nervous wreck within seconds. TALK? Oh God.

Women have this gene that allows them to enjoy talking on a phone for more than two whole minutes, gossiping but exchanging precious little information.

My wife can see her friend all day and then still find something to call her about later that night and talk for over an hour. My friend Kevin won't talk to me at all on the phone if we are due to meet up for fear of having nothing to talk about when we do. This is how it is with men.

Women love to talk, and tell you stuff you don't need to know about people you don't know.

'You know Sheryl, don't you?'

'No, I haven't met her so no point carrying on telling me.'

'Doesn't matter. Her mum is getting these flushes.'

'Right.'

'You listening to me? I always take an interest in what you have to say.'

'Who is Sheryl?'

'Doesn't matter. I can't stand her.'

The talking gene also extends to voicemail messages...

17. THE 20-MINUTE MESSAGE GENE IN WOMEN

A man's voicemail message is a sentence. A woman's is an essay.

I used to routinely delete my wife's messages after 20 seconds of waffle. She would then ask why I didn't pick up the dry cleaning and discover I had never made it that far with her message. She now factors this in by saying 'LISTEN TO THIS MESSAGE DO NOT DELETE IT' at the start of the message.

Only a man has 'comedy' voicemail greetings. I was saddened to call up a friend in the early days of answer machines to find he had made his message over the theme tune to The Professionals. When confronted about this over a few beers he confessed that it took him over two hours to get it right. I forgave him on the spot as only a man would think that a project like that needs good time devoted to it. The worst 'funny' voicemail is the one we've all fallen for – where we are tricked into thinking the other person is there and you start talking to them.

VOICEMAIL MESSAGE: Hi, how are you?

YOU: Ah, you are there, yeah, I'm just calling to –

VOICEMAIL MESSAGE: HA, FOOLED YOU! THIS IS A MESSAGE! HA HA!

You feel really hurt and let down. Confused. It's like being punched in the stomach by the person. Imagine you were calling about a big bit of business. A multi-million-pound deal and you're ringing after your big pitch to say, 'Yes, we're in.' Then you get the comedy message and suddenly you don't feel like you could work with someone who could do that to another person.

Women don't do the comedy message. They do the 'cute' ones. Which are just as bad. Annoying brats saying ,'This is Mummy's phone.' Unless it's my kids and then it's really cute.

A man leaving a message is like he's on a stakeout and can't say too much.

'Hi, be back around seven. Bye.'

From the talking genus also comes the high-pitched gene. During any phone call or greeting of two of more ladies, this gene causes the carrier(s) to shriek a lot.

'Hi, Caaaaaaaaaaaaarool, ooooooooooo!' Dogs have to cover their ears and little green aliens light years away say, 'What the hell was that? Let's not visit there.'

The advent of widespread mobile ownership has made the talking gene in women get stronger and quite frankly worse.

I would now like to appeal to all mobile phone companies to help us men out:

Dear Mr Mobile Phone Company,

Well, I hope you're happy.

Thanks to you, Mr Mobile Phone Company, we can now be contacted 24 hours a day.

It gets worse. We cannot relax on our backsides watching TV without that sodding text alert thing going off as they receive their billionth text that day from their dopey mate they only saw two friggin' hours ago.

Sure, we have benefited too. Without you, Jack Bauer wouldn't have been invented. It's also so much quicker now to bully, insult and harass mates.

But you owe us. Big time. I have worked out how you can start to pay us back.

TREBLE WOMEN'S BILLS AND SEND A SMALL BUT NOTICEABLE ELECTRIC CURRENT THROUGH THEIR HANDSET ON ANY CALL GOING OVER TWO MINUTES. This may act as a deterrent. May.

All men's handsets to come with the following technology as standard: a device fitted that a man can activate to provide fake background noises. Say he is still in the pub, he presses a button and suddenly the sound effects allow him to be on the train with tannoy announcements apologising profusely for the severe delays. The same device can be activated so that when in the company of other men and his other half is on the phone asking/ordering him to say he loves her, he can now save face and technology will convert him saying 'I'LL BE BACK WHEN I GODDAMN FEEL LIKE IT AND WHEN I

AM MAKE SURE YOU HAVE A BACON SARNIE WAITING
FOR ME AND ARE KITTED OUT IN THE SLUTTIEST
UNDERWEAR AS YOU'RE GONNA GET IT' into 'I love
you munchkin bunny woo woos, kiss kiss'.

Yours truly,

All The Men In The World

PS Could you also invent something that we can trigger to
make the phone ring when we are stuck in very dull
conversations.

18. THE BIRTHDAY CARDS/GIFT GENE IN WOMEN

Firstly, women actually bother to remember them. This is due to
the diary gene (see earlier). A man will expect the woman to send
a birthday card to his mum or sister. If this doesn't happen, it
won't be the man's fault:

'I can't believe you forgot my mum's birthday! How could you
do that?'

'Wasn't in the diary.'

Having this gene also means that a woman will keep spare
birthday cards and thank you notes. Most women will have a
small concession of Clintons Cards in a drawer somewhere in the
house. With stamps. (Women always seem to know where the
supply of stamps and Immodium are.) It's thanks to this female
gene that thank you notes and cards are sent out. I remember
after we got married it was my job to post the thank you cards.
I put them in a bottom drawer, with the honest intention of
getting round to it at some point. I really did. Then two years later

we were packing up to move house and my wife found them...
Two years after she left me to post them. The first thing I knew
about this potentially life-threatening discovery was my wife
thrusting them to me silently. You cannot imagine the fallout
from this discovery. I can now blame genetics.

They say many marriages fail in the first few weeks. It's the thank
you card issue. May I take this opportunity to thank my Auntie
Linda for the lovely china cheeseboard?

Before I move on, let me share this bit of wisdom I have learnt
after ten years of marriage:

NEVER UNDERESTIMATE THE IMPORTANCE OF CARDS TO WOMEN

We just pick a card with something that looks nice on the front.
Women care about what's on the inside. What you have written
for them. A card's message is just as, if not more, important as a
present. This I learnt, like many of life's lessons, the hard way.
Picture the scene. It's our tenth wedding anniversary. I have flown
her to Italy. I can do no wrong. Six months of planning. I have just
handed my wife her present. She loves it. There is no gift for me.
It's even better. She enquires where her card is. I say, 'Hang on,
I'll just get it.' This is to buy me some time as I have just realised
it's still in its packet in my bag. Unwritten. I dive into the bag,
grab the card and lock myself in the loo, saying there is
something up with my guts. Romantic, huh?

I rush to write the card. This I now look back on as a VERY BIG
MISTAKE. I make three spelling mistakes that are messily
corrected. One's the spelling of her name. I hand her the card. She

knows I have just written it. On the crapper. It has spelling mistakes. She is not happy. Everything is being eclipsed by Cardgate. The trip to Italy. The fact I got no tenth wedding anniversary present. All the good boy points I was building up for an all-time high score gone. Schoolboy error.

The lesson here?

Cards. Really important. Write them slowly. In pencil first, then ink. Remember her name.

19. THE TOTAL RECALL GENE IN WOMEN

Women never forget, apart from any argument in which you were once right and they were wrong, if that's ever happened. That's immediately forgotten. Discarded to their mind's recycle bin.

Very different when you have been in the wrong. Very different. It's burnt onto their mind's hard drive. Fused to it. Things may move on. Time does heal.

BUT DON'T EVER THINK IT'S FORGOTTEN ABOUT. IT ISN'T.

At some point, it will be brought up again. There is no time limit for our previous convictions. Just as your police record has your misdemeanours listed, that's what women have on us. Every man has form as long as your arm with his partner. Nothing is disregarded. We do something wrong and an instant drop-down menu appears in their heads listing all our other mistakes.

We are never offered probation for our crimes; no chance of getting parole or early release. It's a life sentence.

This gene also helps women bring up in a disagreement something that is in no way related to the current disagreement. You're arguing about ruining her favourite top by putting the wrong wash on. This will be the perfect opportunity to bring up that time eleven years ago when you got so drunk you threw up in the dog's bed. After a dodgy pint. The two are related in their mind. The same person did them. You. That's the connection.

'I'm really sorry about your top, it's just a mistake.'

'Yeah, a mistake from the man who just went to bed once when I was being sick.'

'What?'

'And don't think you're having your boys night out this weekend.'

'But what's that got to do with me getting your top red?'

'As if you don't know.'

I think the government needs to step in with legislation. I think it should be made illegal to bring up anything after six months.

They say many of our wars have been the result of men's lust for power and control. Women say if they were in charge there wouldn't be so many wars. Maybe. Instead of weapons of mass destruction there would be weapons created by women that would just make you feel really bad and tearful. I can just imagine the scene at a UN summit. All is going well among the women from around the world when suddenly Syria brings up something Israel did over 100 years ago.

20. THE POKER FACE GENE IN WOMEN

One of the scariest genes. To present the line 'Let's not get each other presents this year' with utter conviction. It is a bluff. It NEVER means 'Let's not get each other presents this year'.

The poker face comes into play when women use one of the most terrifying words in their arsenal. Only four letters long. F-I-N-E.

Fine never means fine. 'Yeah, don't worry, it's fine.' Fine means 'you're dead'.

Just like when women are really pissed off and yet deny it:

'I'm not angry.'

'You have steam coming out of your ears and are holding a knife to my throat.'

'I'm just a bit disappointed and hurt, not angry.'

'What have I done?'

'What, you need me to spell it out? I shouldn't have to.'

Women expect all men to be Derren Brown-style mind readers who can work out what's wrong by simple brain power.

A man can get through 17 different wives, read umpteen (no idea exactly how many umpteen is but it's always used to mean quite a few, isn't it?) books about relationships and still have no idea what he has done wrong or why his other half is furious. Men are clueless when it comes to reading women.

21. THE SEX AND THE CITY GENE IN WOMEN

Is this the ultimate divide in the male-female chasm? Being able to spend time with Carrie and her self-obsessed hags? Do women really behave like this? How could any sane man like a TV show with a character called Mr Big?

It makes out that all women are obsessed with shoes and swapping intimate physical details about men and our failings. No wonder they like it so much. (Although I'm surprised women like it so much because all the cast are too thin and too good-looking which usually means all other women automatically hate them.)

This show appeals to a unique gene in women and do not trust any man with testicles who says he likes it. He is probably a closet homosexual or in the early stages of a relationship when he will pretend to like anything you do to get in your knickers.

May 28 2008 will be remembered as the worst day for men in years. The day *Sex and the City* was released. Some poor guy rang my radio show saying he was being blackmailed by his wife in the worst possible way. Go to see it with her or there will be no sex in his city. The week this evil – and that is the right word – came out, we became one nation under the thumb. To go and see it.

Simon the cabbie, a regular and very funny caller to my show, rang in with a very important question about the film. If we were the film's producers, what's the best way we could end the movie, making sure they could never return? We had thousands of very graphic and at times disturbing ideas. The best of which are here:

The 'heroes' semi-clad on a fold-up bed – the bed folds back into the wall and they are never found.
Taximan Dan in Stirling

The three look into Sarah Jessica Parker's eyes and turn into stone.
Kenny Mac

Sarah Jessica Parker breaks her ankle with big heels and has to be put down by a vet.
Gabby

Add Sven-Göran Eriksson to the *Sex and the City* management team – ratings would fall and the rot would set in immediately.
Scott

Crossing the road, all four get their Jimmy Choos stuck in a drain grate and are mown down by a garbage truck.
Crazy Pete

A sunbed burns them to a crisp.
Iqbar

The perfect ending to *Sex and the City* – a boardroom and the mighty Sugar man on a slightly raised chair. Sex and the City, you're fired! Nick and Margaret take them outside and slot them with a few double taps!
Little Jason

The Mother Ship returns but the woman driver crashes trying to reverse out of our universe.
Pete

And the best...

All the girls get married and the sex immediately stops then.
Sam

22. THE COLOUR GENE IN WOMEN

The gene to fully appreciate colour and its application exists only
in women. Co-ordinating clothes and tones and shades and
knowing what duck-shell blue is. (My wife has just read that last
line over my shoulder and told me it's actually duck-egg blue. See
what I'm saying?)

Men have a terrible sense of colour. Look at golfers. Most of us
will have bought a shirt or some item of clothing that should
never have left the shop with us. Over the years I have had several
of these. Two things are to blame:

1. Men's lack of the colour gene.

2. Our wives and girlfriends for letting us leave the house
looking the way we do sometimes. Maybe they want us
looking like idiots so that no other women will be attracted
to us.

The colour of towels, sheets and even toilet rolls matter to
women.

I swear men could even be colour-blind. When our first daughter
Ruby was born I was dispatched to John Lewis to get some
Babygros. I wanted so much to get this right as my wife had done
her bit in carrying and giving birth to our beautiful daughter and I
felt like I needed to man up and do what I could.

'Getting the Babygros no problem, darling, leave it to me.' Within the hour, I was back home, mission accomplished. My wife laughed in my face. I thought she would be really impressed as I had actually bought three as they were on a special deal.

'They're blue,' she pointed out.

'Yes. And?'

'We have a daughter. That means pink.'

'How do we know she doesn't like blue as well?'

'TAKE THEM BACK.'

I took them back and explained my little mistake to the lady in the store and that I wished to swap them for some pink ones. She said she had to check with her supervisor. She walked over to her and after a few moments they were both looking at me and laughing. It's ugly discrimination I experienced that day. I can't help my lack of genes. Sure, I understand now that blue is for boys and pink is for girls. I have it written down in my wallet. I'm not stupid.

This genetic disability men suffer from, and suffer is the right word, has caused many of us to screw up when loading the washing machine. Women laugh at us and accuse us of being lazy or incompetent but we are genetically disadvantaged because we do not have the colour gene. We need a warning card in our wallets like people with nut allergies or diabetes.

We either use the wrong programme (is there another one other than the classic and timeless 40 degrees quick wash?) or mix our favourite old red T-shirt with her newly purchased white blouse. These washing machines must be made by man-hating lesbians. They are simply not man-friendly. They need to come voice activated like KITT in Knightrider.

Despite our lack of prowess in this area (our mums didn't help by doing everything for us), if it breaks down it's always a man who comes to repair it. The washing machine MAN. Most repair people are men. We like fiddling and repairing things. Not using them correctly so much. But tinkering, great. In fact, if women used our natural love of tinkering more they could get a better quality of foreplay. Less about 'caress me' and more about 'tinker with me' and simpering, 'I'm broken, repair me...' Just don't go too far with this and tell her you're going to take a look under her hood and then bang your hand on her to try and get her running again. And don't wash your hands with Swarfega afterwards.

This newspaper headline proves what I'm saying:

> Leeds Man Laundered Stolen Money in Washing Machine
>
> A LEEDS man tried to clean coloured dye from £60,000 of stolen money by putting it in a washing machine
>
> *Yorkshire Evening Post*, April 2008

You can imagine him ringing his mum to try and get her advice on the best wash to put it on.

One sure way to get an argument going is to go through a paint colour chart together. Your eyes just don't see the same thing. I remember my dad almost having some kind of meltdown when he was decorating our front room. My mum couldn't decide on the colour and I'm not kidding had over ten different patches on one wall from those little paint pots. She settled on one and my dad did the room as instructed. She hated it and picked another colour. I swear I heard him sobbing silently as he got his brushes and turps (only dads are allowed to use turps) out again.

A final colour word of warning, guys. If you're single, never buy dark sheets as women find them creepy. Only Peter Stringfellow has dark bed linen. And it shows up stains. You know the ones.

23. THE 'IT REALLY IS JUST A GAME' GENE IN WOMEN

Women have the gene to put sport into perspective. Men cannot. This is why football managers are men. Otherwise the half-time chat wouldn't be the classic Sir Alex Ferguson hairdryer treatment. It would be a calm chat, making sure all the players felt appreciated. Chatting about each other's feelings and being sent back out for the second half after being told, 'Don't worry, it's just a game. *Dancing On Ice* is on later so cheer up.'

This gene is the reason why many women see no problem in starting up a conversation while you're watching sport on TV. For some reason, many even start to suddenly get horny the moment they hear the *Match of the Day* theme tune. Funny that.

The game of the century between Chelsea and Manchester United in the European Cup Final. Edge-of-the-seat stuff that goes to the vicious cruelness of the penalty shootout. You're not going anywhere. To my wife, it was the perfect moment to ask me to move our suitcases into the loft.

I remember when Southampton got relegated from the Premiership. It was like part of my childhood dying. I can't say I went to every home game but I was seriously down. The team that gave the world legends like Mick Channon, Peter Shilton and the godlike Le Tissier relegated. The world seemed a very unfair place that day. The thought of clashes against Preston North End and Hull was like when Ali came out of retirement and got beaten by Larry Holmes. My wife looked at me and suggested I pick a new team.

24. THE SEEING GENE IN WOMEN

I'm big on the theory that there are major design problems with men's eyes. We have serious medical conditions. We lack the seeing gene that women have. Women have hawk-like vision. They notice that something is dirty, needs replacing or is in the wrong place. Then another gene kicks in which we also seem to lack. The 'do something about it' gene. Men have the 'ignore it' gene in abundance.

This is why only women should operate the X-ray machines at airport security. Men zone out because they're not as nosy as women and get bored quickly. Women want to know what's in the bags and can notice things better due to their genetic make-up. A man sees bomb-making equipment and won't really want to say anything to cause a scene. Too much hassle and fuss.

My wife puts things on the bottom of the stairs for one of us to take the next time we go up. That's how she sees it anyway. I simply see things which need to be stepped over to continue on my journey upstairs. Until I am told/ordered otherwise, I assume she's having a bit of fun making a little obstacle course for me.

Men are aware and in awe of this all-seeing power. That's why, out of respect and for no other reason, we will always bow down to women's prowess and ask 'where is the cheese?' while putting our face in the fridge less than two inches from the very cheese we are looking for. I have lost count of the times I have asked my wife, 'Where is my shirt?' which will be right in front of me in the wardrobe. Or on me.

Their Achilles heel is keys. Most of my waking life is spent looking for my wife's house or car keys. For some reason these are always being lost. It is usually somehow my fault too. 'You must have moved them' is the reward I get for finding them.

25. THE 'IN A MINUTE' GENE IN MEN

Men possess the 'In a minute/I was just about to do that' gene. The very moment we are reminded for the ninth time to do something and then we see our other half doing it to make a point, we leap out of our seat as if 20,000 volts has passed into us, yelling, 'I was just about to do that!' while chomping on a crisp sandwich.

The 'In a minute' sub-gene is related to the above. It's a response to persistent nagging, like one of those automatic email replies. It's fired off reflexively. We feel it will get done in due time, our time. Man time. For some reason, if a man is watching something important on TV like *The Deadliest Catch*, he cannot even think about doing anything until it's finished. Even then he will need some time to fully take in what he has just seen, especially if it's a MacGyver repeat.

26. THE BULLSHIT GENE IN MEN

Only found in men because men are born bullshitters. Put any man in a difficult situation and he will fall back to his default setting. Lying. Bill Clinton gets caught throwing his man juice over a chubby intern and it's 'I did not have sexual relations with that woman.'

From our schooldays to adult life, men lie. A friend of mine was in a bar, getting on really well with a girl, and at the end of the night she said it would be nice if he called her. He then panicked as he realised he had forgotten her name. Now, he could have just told her and laughed it off. But because he's a man with a bullshit gene, he didn't. He did this. He calmly took his phone out and opened up the address book. He then slowly and drunkenly said, 'So how do you spell it then...'

This little game went on for a few letters until she caught on. Women can smell the bull gene and she rumbled him and walked off.

I remember many years ago a friend of mine waking up and not knowing who the girl in bed next to him was. No idea. She said she would cook them breakfast and he was in the kitchen when the way out of this mess presented itself to him. He saw some post on the table. Smart guy, he thought, he would use this 'intel' just like a secret agent. He used the name. She stopped cooking and informed him that was her flatmate's name. 'Taxi!'

No, the thing to do is hand her the phone and get her to put her number in herself. (I know this because someone once called my radio show with this nugget for all the wannabe George Clooneys out there.)

27. THE MARKED DOWN GENE IN WOMEN

While men have the bullshit gene, women have their own version – the marked down gene. Where any purchased item will be marked down by £30 or more. By them. So you think, Wow, what a bargain you got there – smart move buying them at such a low price. If they weren't so damn cheap, you wouldn't have got them, right? Right?

This has an added advantage. Despite you knowing she's lying, if you are smart you go along with the lie. She knows what you are doing and you feel this gameness on your part not to kick off about the real cost of the shoes may get you some later. It's a win-win. If things don't go to plan later, then you have no choice but to bring up this quite frankly shocking deceit that is bigger than just lying about the cost of the shoes. Again, do this right and you could get the happy ending you wanted. You just have to lay the bait with total conviction and no hint of an erection.

'If you could lie about the shoes, what else could you lie about? I mean, do I even know you?'

Do it quietly, not angrily or shouting. You are more hurt than anything else. Get it right and she tries to console you – and women know how best to console a hurt man. Through his penis. Do not be too quick to accept the fandango offering. But do accept it.

Don't ever ask for the receipt as they get angry when challenged on this lie. Like a cornered animal, they will lash out at you and you could lose an eye.

This gene is balanced by a similar one in men, which we come to next.

28. THE MARK UP GENE IN MEN

Part of the bullshit gene family, this gene is more specific. This gene is the reason men 'mark up' time. For example, a man is in the pub and is called by his wife:

Woman: When are you leaving as you said you'd be home soon, and that was an hour ago?

Man: Just leaving now. Martin turned up and he's a bit upset as the doctor has told him he has a rare tropical illness and will die screaming in pain.

Woman: My God! Poor Marty, I should call his wife.

Man: NO. You mustn't. She doesn't know yet. Let poor Marty do that in his own time.

Now, several genes are actually in play here. The bullshit gene as Marty is fine but needed to be sacrificed to prevent a row. Secondly, the woman's talking gene as her immediate response was to get on the fucking phone. Thirdly, the 'marked up' gene when the man said he was leaving now. The concept of 'now' is exactly the same as when women shout they are ready 'now' when they still have at least another hour before that's true as they haven't put their mascara on yet. With men the 'now' actually means after the next round, or one after that. They have 'marked up' the real time departure.

29. THE CRUELLEST LIE GENE IN WOMEN

This gene is a nasty one and has been used on many of us. This little story will illustrate just how strong and deceptive it is.

One afternoon after a particular hearty lunch, myself and my radio producers headed to a nearby pub for a few drinks. Sambucas were ordered to 'liven things up'. Being wild and crazy guys, we agreed we all had to be done by 5pm or we'd start getting the calls asking us what time we were leaving and then it would be playtime over.

As the drinks were flowing, one of the gathered was chatting about his new girlfriend. He then boasted about something she had said to him. This caused me to laugh so hard I spat my drink out of my mouth and I think a little bit of wee came out too. He had been told the biggest lie a woman can say to a man. It's also the cruellest lie, as every man who has ever been told it believes it.

You will now be wondering what the lie is. I'm not sure you really want to know. If I tell you, nothing will ever be the same again. You will question yourself, your previous partners and current ones. You will disregard what I am about to tell you and say to yourself you are the exception as in your case it's not a lie. It's true. That's the thing with this great lie. We all believe it. We want it to be true.

What is the biggest and cruellest lie a women can ever say to a man?

You're the best? No.

You have an amazing body? No.

You're the funniest man I have ever met? No.

No, the lie is:

'YOURS IS THE BIGGEST I HAVE EVER SEEN' and 'IT'S MUCH BIGGER THAN MY EX'S'

Think it through. Everything is spinning right now and you're about to drop this very book. Like in The Usual Suspects when the detective finally puts it all together about Keyser Sose. I'm sorry I had to be the one to tell you.

My friend in the bar denied that it was a lie just as you are doing right now. 'No, I've seen a picture of him on Facebook and he's a right short-arse.' Again my drink was sprayed. Is height a measure of a man's cock? Poor Tom Cruise.

30. THE STINK EYE GENE IN WOMEN

Men fear it. The juju curse that's been around for generations. A woman can give a 17 stone hard man a single look that could strike a fear previously unknown into him.

The stink eye is the look that lasts no more than a millisecond yet it is the glare that goes into your soul then winds round your balls and squeezes them. And your throat. Causing your heart rate to increase dramatically and all colour to drain from your face. Your bum will also start to squeak.

No word is said. It doesn't need to be. You know immediately you are in clear and present danger. You better have your story straight as hell is about to be unleashed upon you. Most of us just want to drop to our knees and beg for our lives upon getting 'the eye' but that would only make it worse. Like dogs, they smell fear. (I'm not in any way suggesting there is a connection between canines and women – I'm just looking for an example in the animal world.)

Shouting, swear words and insults are nothing compared to the silence and the stink eye. Sometimes it's waiting for you the moment the front door is opened. Sometimes you can be at a social engagement and you bring something up that's embarrassing for your partner. You get the Stink-atollah. It's the mark of death. It cannot be retracted. Other men can see it and give you an early warning: 'Your missus is giving you the stink eye... want me to get the spare room ready?' At school our chemistry teachers told us plutonium was the most dangerous. They lied. It's the stink eye. Should be on that table, after the transition elements.

31. THE NINJA GENE IN WOMEN

Women have the ninja gene where they can eye up a fine-looking man without being noticed, using their ninja powers. They have the periphery vision powers to be discreet. Men simply do not. Even when we are standing right in front of someone, our heads are bowed, mouth agape, eyes staring at the breasts of the woman we are talking to. We might as well just reach out and grab them, it's that unsubtle. Men don't possess the subtle gene either.

It's like staring at the sun – you want to but you really shouldn't. You can try what I call the 'Action Man' technique, which can only be used when wearing sunglasses. Your head looks ahead but your eyes, just like the eyes on an Action Man, see what you want to see. Be careful, though – maybe the reason Action Man had no genitals is because his missus caught him and ripped them off.

Perhaps some men just get confused as to where women's faces are.

A woman can enter a room and within seconds have scanned it. She will have clocked the fit men and the women who are a threat and may need neutralising.

Women may not be aware that control of our eyes can be taken by our penis. You can be having a very pleasant chat to your other half and then something walks by, with legs and breasts. You know it's rude to look at other women so you don't, but then your penis hears about this woman walking by and it hijacks our eyes. It only has the one itself.

A woman can walk past a man and he won't even know he's been eyed up. This happens to me every day. I walk past stunning women and they don't even bat an eyelid. But I know they are mentally undressing me. A man can't eye up a woman without it being very obvious. He usually walks into a lamppost or oncoming traffic. This behaviour is of course down to his genes. Specifically the next one.

32. THE EASILY DISTRACTED GENE IN MEN

Men get easily distracted. Men get even more distracted by provocatively dressed women. One London law firm has even gone as far as taking things back to the Victorian times:

LEGAL FIRM BANS FISHNET STOCKINGS

BECAUSE THEY DISTRACT MALE COLLEAGUES

When we are driving, this easily distracted gene can be dangerous. While conducting my research for this book, I came across more evidence of this:

'Male drivers easily distracted – survey'

Male drivers are more likely to be distracted by reading a newspaper, kissing or chasing insects while driving a car than women.

News.com.au

Firstly, what man reads a newspaper and drives? (Unless you drive a National Express coach.) And I for one have never 'kissed or chased an insect' while driving my car.

33. THE WOLF-WHISTLING GENE IN MEN

This isn't in all men but mainly men in white vans. Maybe it's the van that activates this gene. Men in white vans have to operate a two-man system to protect the driver and his easily distracted mind (see earlier gene). One acts as lookout and alerts the driver to any attractive ladies and he then toots the horn while his wingman shouts out, 'Phwoar!', the classic 'Oi oi!', or wolf-whistles.

Then they get upset when the lady doesn't show any sign of appreciation for this. Lesbian, they decide. I often wonder if any woman in history has ever said, when asked how she met the love of her life, 'He was leaning out of a Transit van and shouted "Oi oi darling" at me. I saw him, the empty Greggs wrappers in the van window, and knew, right then and there, he was the one.'

34. THE 'WHAT ARE YOU THINKING?' GENE IN WOMEN

Women are more inquisitive than men. Or just plain nosy. My wife is always eavesdropping on other people's conversations. I'm surprised MI5 don't use her as some kind of remote monitoring station for suspected terrorist activity.

Women want and need to know what we are thinking, all the time. Now this cannot be because we are deep thinkers. Wise sages who regularly dispense pearls of wisdom. No.

The real problem here is that women think we are actually thinking in the first place. When we all know we rarely are. I just asked my wife the same question, and she said,

'Your mum coming up to stay tomorrow and do the sheets need changing on the bed in the spare room? What are the kids going to eat tonight for tea? The party we have been invited to this Friday and what should I wear? What we are going to do for Christmas this year and is your sister really pissed off at not being asked to be a godparent?'

She then asked me the same thing.

'Nothing.'

Women are always thinking about things, sometimes while we are having sex with them. Then they will be thinking about the sheets in the dryer.

But what do men really think about? I wrote down my thoughts over a ten-minute period.

Sex

Do pets have open casket funerals? Could Digby my wonder dog have one? I think it would be nice

Nothing

Sex

If Colombo and Inspector Morse were put on the same case, who would crack it first?

What's my favourite sandwich?

Why did my wife not get me any more pickled onions?

Sex

Staring at pigeons wondering if I really did see one wink at another

Nothing

So you see how it's a lottery what I may be thinking at any given moment. My wife couldn't handle the real dull truth.

I suggest you just rotate the following three standard answers to help yourself:

The first time we met (Always works)

How lovely petals are

Nothing

35. THE SHOEBOX GENE IN WOMEN

Collecting photos and old love letters in shoeboxes. Women naturally do this. Photos are very important to them. Men like to have photos of their loved ones on their desks at work. I think it was Jerry Seinfeld who said this is to remind them they have a family and not to get blow jobs after work but head home.

The shoebox gene relates to the collecting and storage of nice bags too. My wife has a special bag to keep other carrier bags in. I do too. It's called the bin bag. Women need to keep a check on this gene as it can turn them into that bag lady every town had. You don't see too many scary bag ladies these days; most have been employed in health food shops.

The shoebox gene can mutate into a form where various articles are cut out of magazines and kept. For what purpose is never made clear.

36. THE CATATONIC GENE IN WOMEN

Even if a woman gets 30 hours sleep a day, she will still be tired upon waking.

Also, women will always have the monopoly on the right to feel the most tired. Even if you have climbed the Himalayas and then walked all the way home with no shoes on, they will still be more tired that you. YOU CAN NEVER WIN THE WHO'S MORE TIRED FIGHT WITH A WOMAN. EVER.

37. THE SHOPPING GENE IN WOMEN

I like shopping. For about 24 minutes. I managed to get myself a new pair of shoes in under 90 seconds online. Job done. However, one thing you don't want to shop for online is shoes. They turn up in your normal size but they don't seem to fit humans. This was a mistake. Not that I'm telling my wife that. That would mean admitting I was wrong and we don't do that.

Men on the whole do not like shopping. It is not in our genes. The stores know this, which is why the men's department is usually on the ground floor near the exits.

It is technically impossible for a man and a woman to spend the entire day shopping together without some kind of argument breaking out. Unless:

1. There is the promise of sex at the end of it all.

2. The man is fed and watered regularly. A hungry man is a stroppy man.

3. He is gay.

4. He has been chemically castrated.

5. He is dead.

The shopping gene is a strong one in women. Even my three-year-old daughter Ruby loves going shopping. Men see it as something to get done as quickly as possible. Speed-shopping is what we prefer.

When I go shopping with my wife exactly the same thing always happens.

We got to a shop, she sees something she really likes.

She tries it on. I slump in the allocated man chair, losing the will to live despite only have been shopping for seven minutes.

She comes out from the dressing room seeking my opinion.

Guess what?

I love it.

'Buy it. BUY IT NOW. PLEASE SAVE MY SOUL. THE LIGHTING AND AIR CONDITIONING ARE KILLING ME. YES I REALLY LIKE IT. NO REALLY LIKE. I LIKE IT. I'M NOT JUST SAYING THAT. IT'S THE BEST THING I HAVE EVER SEEN IN MY FUCKING LIFE. I'M COMING JUST LOOKING AT IT. GIVE IT TO ME. I'LL GO AND BUY IT NOW...'

We of course don't buy it. We visit another 376 shops.

Then go back to the first one and buy it.

38. THE 'AFTER THE LIGHTS GO OUT' GENE IN WOMEN

Women are genetically predisposed to believing that when the lights go out and you start to nod off it is the precise moment you should commence a full-blown conversation about a major life issue.

Just this week after saying good night there was the dreaded pause followed by an audible intake of breath from my wife and...

'Do you think we should change the mortgage?'

My favourite ever late-night chat, after which I couldn't actually sleep for laughing, was, and I swear I'm not making this up:

> 'You must remind me to have a conversation with
> my_____(FAMILY MEMBER'S IDENTITY DELETED DUE TO
> WIFE GIVING ME THE STINK EYE) about her stools.'

Just so you know, not stools as in furniture.

39. THE FIVE-MINUTE GENE IN WOMEN

As we have already discussed, neither sexes perceive time in the same way but women really have more of a problem. Specifically the five-minute gene.

This can cover many areas:

Five minutes... and I'll be ready to leave.

IT IS NEVER FIVE MINUTES. Take your jacket and shoes off and sit your arse back on the couch.

Five minutes... that's all we are popping in to see my mum for. Just for five minutes. *You'll be there all afternoon and all the old photos will be coming out. Don't roll your eyes like that looking at your watch either or extra time is added on.*

Five minutes... is all it'll take getting some new bed linen in this shop.
Start running now.

40. THE 'RAT DOG' GENE IN WOMEN

Think about the great dogs of TV and film. Lassie, the Littlest Hobo, K9, Hooch, Columbo's one simply called 'Dog', Mel Gibson's in the Lethal Weapon films. Every single one of them a proper dog. Not a manky little rat-like thing that can do nothing. No man has any business owning a dog that:

- can be easily carried under an arm

- can be dressed in silly little outfits

- yaps instead of barks

My dog Digby isn't a big dog but none of the above apply to him and he has a real dog bark even if it is at the snooker on TV sometimes.

Incidentally this gene is the one responsible for the cat love too. A man pretends to love a cat then kicks it when you're out the room. Cats get their own back and deliberately hiss at you and women start to think the cat has picked up on something about you. I know a woman who lets her cat vet her boyfriends. The cat doesn't like them, that's it. Cats are shits. Mark my words.

41. THE 42-INCH GENE IN MEN

Men are genetically programmed to have the need to own and love a 42-inch plasma screen. I mean really love. They may even keep a picture of it in their wallet. Or on their desk at work. If those things could perform oral sex it could be over for women.

It's the first thing a man would want to show off to another man. Forget the loft conversion. Look at the picture quality on this baby...

Actually men love showing off any gadgets and hardware. Even the greatest Bond baddie ever Blofeld came undone with this genetic weakness. He couldn't help but show Bond all the stuff that was going to end the world. If he hadn't had this gene he would have just lasered big Sean's old fella.

42. THE MANESIA GENE IN MEN

Men forget things. I have just finished reading a report headlined 'Men More Forgetful Than Women' from the American Academy of Neurology. It says men are 'one-and-a-half times more likely to have mild cognitive impairment than women'.

Maybe it's because men have to remember important information like the offside rule and which Bond movie Nick Nack is in and our team's FA Cup record. This means there just isn't too much memory space left for stuff like significant others' birthdays and anniversary dates, etc, etc.

The manesia gene is no laughing matter. I can be dispatched to the shops for bread and return with a packet of Tunnock's Tea Cakes and Mint Viscounts (they were out of Boasters) but no bread. I will be totally clueless as to what happened. It's as if Derren Brown has done some mind meld on me.

This manesia gene may be another reason why some men have affairs. They think one woman looks very similar to their partner in that she also has breasts and a face.

43. THE SCREENSAVE FACE GENE IN MEN

This gene is in all men and it enables us to go into a 'safe' mode while in conversation with your other half about how her day went. Sometime around the 38th minute of her indepth account, like a computer with a period of inactivity, your man 'screensave' face kicks in.

You zone out to Man Land. It's a journey they can't really come on and at any moment you can be brought crashing down to earth with a 'you haven't heard a word I've just said, have you?'. That's when this next man gene can save you.

44. THE KEY WORDS GENE IN MEN

The key word gene has helped many men out of a possible firefight that could postpone or cancel any previously approved man time or bedroom fun. All leave is cancelled if this gene doesn't take over and do the heavy lifting.

Men and how we 'hear' a conversation is very similar to an internet search. I wouldn't be surprised if the amazing way we selectively hear was what Google was built upon.

Men hear certain key words in a conversation. That's why if you are suddenly confronted with the 'What did I just say then...?' challenge, the key word gene will allow a man to reel off some of the key words that have been temporally stored.

'I heard everything... your mum... her hair... cat... sick... double-parked.'

It's like *The Generation Game*. The game ends badly though if they aren't impressed with these mental gymnastics and push you for the D word. Detail. The natural enemy of men.

'What else? Come on, what else did I say?'

That's when you're fucked.

If they had worked with our key word gene and inserted words that catch our man minds, then we could all get on much better. Words that pertain to:

Sex

Food

Us

'And then the cashier had to do a price check and THREESOME
the supervisor told me that I could have them TITS for nothing.
Sheila was there and was wearing BEER those new shoes I want a
pair of. Can you BLOW JOB put the rubbish out?'

45. THE WILL WATCH ALMOST ANYTHING ON TV GENE IN MEN*

I will not be in the same postcode as any TV showing *Sex and the
City* or any reality show centred around musicals. But I'm more
than happy to watch, in my wife's words, 'crap like this'. The 'this'
she was talking about happened to be one of the greatest TV
shows ever.

Animal Face Off. I found this by accident while channel surfing.
The idea is sheer genius. If two animals had a fight, who would
win? You know only a man could have come up with an idea like
that. I'm guessing alcohol was involved and at a point where
someone had someone else in a headlock, that someone suddenly
said, well, slurred, more likely, 'Hey, you guys, what if a lion and a
tiger had a fight, who would win?' This is why the world needs us.
Men ask the big important questions. Like WHO WOULD WIN
IN A FIGHT BETWEEN A HIPPO AND A SHARK?

Now, obviously they couldn't use real-life animals. That would be
wrong and immoral (but TV gold... no, it would be WRONG). So
they used mechanical replicas and scientists. The episode I first
chanced upon was a battle royale between a hippo and a bull

---

* *Apart from reality shows/period drama with men in breeches and
lots of people walking around large gardens on crunchy gravel/
anything featuring Davina McCall shouting*

shark. I nodded off before the final result. If anybody knows, please let me know.

I of course became addicted. Who couldn't fall for the charms of match-ups like:

Polar Bear vs Walrus

(Toe-to-toe action with the fight going both ways before the final telling blow. I found myself oddly moved to tears by the bravery of these majestic metallic beasts.)

Gorilla vs Leopard

(I won't ruin it for you but the leopard's night vision did give it an early advantage. The ending proved to be a huge upset for fight fans all over the globe.)

Sperm Whale vs Colossal Squid

(A fight where one of the antagonists uses bursts of sound to deadly effect.)

How this never got any BAFTAs I'll never know.

46. THE NAGGING GENE IN WOMEN

Men don't like being hassled. But to be honest we do need prompting because of our genetic failings and design faults, and we have much on our minds: relegation, who'd win in a fight between Asterix and Tintin, and how does Lembit Opik know he's got into the right Cheeky Girl's bed if he's had a few?

My wife tells me she wouldn't have to nag if I did as I was told. Genetics like manesia make it hard for men to remember what we were supposed to do. Which is why we just sit on the couch so much. Men need adult supervision. We forget things easily, switch off, shut down, and zone out. We'd nag if we were in a relationship with someone who did all that. Though it can go too far:

> 'Wife's nagging left me impotent'
>
> An Italian man is demanding £140,000 in compensation after claiming his wife's constant nagging left him impotent

This story from Ananova is about a man called Sergio who has apparently 'produced medical evidence in court' to back up his claims.

What kind of evidence? we ask. Pictures of his flaccid member, looking sorry for itself? Tapes of his wife nagging him and then him crying in the bedroom, claiming that all that nagging about putting the recycling bins out on the right day has left him woodless? What kind of lawyer do you go to about that? One of those one you see in very cheaply made TV adverts shown mainly during daytime telly? The ones about falling off a ladder at work?

47. THE MUSICAL HATRED GENE IN MEN

If you have just started a relationship with someone and are still in that early phase when you actually make an effort to engage in the things they like, then by all means attend a musical. Otherwise, let's be honest, men have a genetic hatred of musicals. Stage musicals.

Cats, Les Mis, Phantom, I feel sick just writing their names. These things have less plot than a Steven Seagal straight-to-DVD special. They go on for hours. With no explosions. On top of this we now have to endure these TV shows on every sodding Saturday night, trying to recruit new members for these horrors.

'How do you solve a problem like Maria?' WHO GIVES A SHIT? 'I'd do anything.' What, even Andrew Lloyd Webber?

The apocalypse is here, people, in our front rooms every Saturday night. Women love them, men have to watch them. We need special contact lenses where it looks like we are watching this crap but really we can see *The Sopranos*. Come on, Apple, hurry up and invent them. After you've solved a problem like Maria, with a crossbow.

48. THE POTTY TIME GENE IN MEN

Men are genetically programmed to enjoy quality toilet time in the loo. It's like a little library and gentleman's club in there. There has to be something to read. Not a *Homes and Interiors* magazine which has been planted in there to brainwash you. The door is locked and like Mr Ben during his lunchbreak, we are taken away from the world outside.

The locking of it annoys our partners. 'Why is this door locked? What are you doing in there?' they demand to know. What exactly could we be up to in there? Having an affair with someone who sneaks in and out from behind the U-bend? Tunnelling out?

Women like to spend time on the phone. Men like to spend time on the throne.

49. THE BATHROOM GENE IN WOMEN

Just how many products does one woman need in her toilet? Your stuff is shoved somewhere away from all of hers in case it touches it. Hidden away. Unless of course it's your razor, which she will use on her legs but not tell you so the next time you go to have a shave it will be blunt and cut your face to shreds. It's manocide.

I rarely use shampoo but when I do it's just that. Shampoo. One bottle. Not five or six. Conditioners. Strengthening conditioners. For combination hair. Vitamin enriched. With aloe vera. What is that stuff? Whoever discovered it must be the world's richest man. It's everywhere. Did the same person also discover tea tree oil? Maybe you need the intense repair shampoo? Sorry, the intense repair nutrition shampoo. Or absolute repair shampoo?

Or hydro resist? Don't you hate hydros when you're washing your barnet and wish there was some way of stopping them? Or better still *resisting them?*

50. THE MANWIDTH GENE IN MEN

To women, communication between men looks like barely noticeable nods and mumbles broken up with long silences. It's far more complicated that that.

Men have a genetically evolved, highly complex communication system with their mates, which still hasn't been fully understood to this day. My field studies have for the first time uncovered the full extent of this ancient system.

MALE COMMUNICATION – THE ESSENTIALS

There are well over 400 different types of nods a man can give, ranging from one towards the bar when it's time for a refill to agreeing with the question 'Shall we go for a curry?'

- 87 different meanings for 'uh huh'

- 34 different types of awkward silences

- 31,873 different mumbles

To the untrained eye, it just looks like some monkeys sitting together grunting.

51. THE FARTS ARE FUNNY GENE IN MEN

This obviously only exists in men. I have never seen a grown woman, when with other women, break wind then waft the pungent aroma towards her mates' vicinity. Doesn't happen.

Only men and children find farting funny.

To men, the watershed moment when they know they are really in a serious relationship is when the farting in bed taboo has been broken. Literally.

Men can mistake the genetic fondness they have for an eggy puff to thinking both sexes enjoy it equally. Which may explain this:

Office worker awarded £5,000 after boss constantly broke wind in her direction

A bullied office worker has been awarded £5,000 after her boss raised his right buttock from his chair and broke wind in her direction.

Metro, 16 May 2008

If you are laughing right now you are a man.

52. THE GRANDSTANDING GENE IN MEN

Sadly men are genetically disposed to make a very big deal when they do anything. 'Hey, babe, I've just emptied the bins... DA DAH' and then wait for a big thank you or applause. 'I've just picked my clothes up and then wiped my own backside' is the equivalent to us finding a cure for the common cold. We expect to be carried around the house on your shoulders.

53. THE LUCKY PANTS GENE IN MEN

Women fail to understand the deal with this gene. It's a contract for life. A man and his underwear of choice. Stronger than the wire they use on kids' toys that you can never cut with scissors or very sharp knives. It's a bond for life. A man and his lucky pants.

They are not just pants. They are magical pants. Like the Dad Pants mentioned elsewhere in this book, they give the wearer special powers. A man is very loyal to and protective of his lucky pants.

Over the years the pants will fray and start showing bald elastic patches around the waistband and offer little in the way of ball support. They look more like museum exhibits from another century. That's not the point. You have other pants that can do all that, but they're not yet lucky. Pants get lucky pant status by being worn when something very good happens. They are then forever seen as some magical garment regardless of smell or the fact they no longer hold your balls in.

Mine are the ones I got married in some ten years ago. Several times they have survived my wife's random and terrifying putsches. She says the pants look tatty, smell funny and have grown bacteria with their own advanced ecosystem. But I could never throw them away.

If lucky pants are binned it's as if our magic man powers have been thrown away with them. We are Superman and all around us is kryptonite. They are not just lucky pants, they provide the wearer with an impenetrable forcefield. That's why they smell like that.

54. THE 'I'LL JUST HAVE SOME OF YOURS' GENE IN WOMEN

How many times have you been in a restaurant and the woman you're with opts for the salad? Your heart drops. You know she'll be stealing your food within seconds of it turning up. It's calorie transfer. If she doesn't actually order it, she can't get the calories – they are yours. So make sure you order enough for two.

The phrase 'just get what you want and I'll have some of that' is bad news as the curry you were looking forward to will be pilfered and you'll be lucky to get three mouthfuls.

One idea might be to deliberately order something foul-tasting, and the lesson will be learned that you order badly. That tip alone is worth this book's modest cover price.

55. THE MAN FLU GENE IN MEN

Women don't understand. Man flu is the most terrifying illness known to mankind. It's not a cold. That's what women get.

If you are taken by man flu there is little you can do to ease your pain and torment. THERE IS NO CURE FOR MAN FLU.

You will spend your last few hours screaming to your inevitable death. Ask for prayers and get your affairs in order. Scientists have yet to develop anything that can come anywhere near killing man flu.

If you are struck by man flu, there are several things you need to do immediately:

- Tell anyone in earshot, 'I think I'm coming down with something'

- Turn on the TV and grab the remote

- Retire to the nearest couch and lie down, ensuring you can see the TV

- Take temperature. When it doesn't show your temperature at 1007 degrees, say 'Damn thing's broken, maybe I did it with my man flu'

- Demand tomato soup and Lucozade

- Start talking about 'going towards the light' and saying, 'No, I'm not ready yet'

● Take temperature again. It's still broken if it's showing normal

● Tell your wife or girlfriend it is not 'just a cold'

● When she laughs, don't get angry. Just calmly and meekly, that's if you can even speak, say, 'If I don't wake up from this kip, remember I love you. Bury me in my lucky pants'

How to deal with a man taken by man flu

This is a handy guide to give to your other half. Advise her to have it nearby at all times or keep it in your wallet to hand to her should you get hit by this deadly virus.

DO:

• REPEATEDLY SAY 'YOU POOR THING, SO BRAVE, I COULD NEVER KNOW OF SUCH PAIN DESPITE BEARING OUR THREE CHILDREN'

• LIE ABOUT THE TEMPERATURE READING. IT'S ALWAYS 'YOU'RE VERY HOT, SHOULD BE DEAD REALLY'

• MAKE SURE THE BED OR COUCH HAS NICELY PLUMPED PILLOWS

DON'T:

• EVER SAY 'YOU HAVE THAT COLD I HAD. TAKE SOME PARACETAMOL'

OR 'I HAD THIS AND STILL LOOKED AFTER THE HOUSE AND OUR KIDS'

• EXPECT ANY SHORT-TERM RECOVERY

My wife once showed me something in a newspaper saying men take on average three days to get over flu. Women half that time. Proof to me they don't get man flu.

56. THE SALES GENE IN WOMEN

For women this gene starts with enjoying a jumble sale with their mum when they were young. They make their first kill here and get the bloodlust. Maybe an old Soda Stream for 50p.

Then it moves on to the horrors of car boot sales. Which they also enjoy way more than men. Buying all kinds of crap which they justify with the words 'I can't believe this was only three quid!' as they hold up some hideous ceramic tat which will never ever be used. Women love to think they have got an amazing bargain. Fortune and the gods have smiled down and shown their existence in the world with this manky crock of shitolla.

Worse than the January/Easter/summer/autumn/spring sales put together is the online version of a car boot sale: eBay.

Now I have got some amazing stuff from eBay. Drunk. A shirt that was very much sold as being worn by Tony Soprano. It was huge and the seller had written on it in marker pen 'bada bing'. Genius. All for only £100.

But my wife is addicted to the thing. The postman is forever bringing us junk she's 'luckily' won on eBay or I'm driving round to complete strangers' houses, saying, 'I'm here for the sink.'

Please make it stop.

57. THE PMT GENE IN MEN

It's not the same, biologically speaking. We don't menstruate,
though I have had a few bosses where I did think they did. But we
get the sudden change in mood and behaviour.

Men's PMT is Pre-Match Tension.

Had it bad before Southampton's last match of the season. If they
lost it meant the unthinkable. Being relegated from the
Championship. Only a win would save them.

I can get really bad man PMT during World Cups and
internationals. When England failed to qualify for Euro 2008
millions of men went to work the next day depressed and
emotional. Not wanting to even 'talk about it'.

58. THE CAR GENE IN MEN

I read a report saying that men will say their car is their most
treasured possession. Women say a photograph of a special
occasion.

A man can love a car; we are born this way. It's true. They did
these studies with male rhesus monkeys. The University of
Atlanta gave a group of young monkeys some dumper trucks, cars
and dolls. The women monkeys had no interest in the cars and
the male ones did.

Women name their cars and they are an extension of their
handbags. Another place to store crap.

Men LOVE their cars. It's easy to understand why. They come with
manuals which are one of the few manuals men bother to read.

They never ask you where you have been. Or laugh at your dress sense. Sure, maintenance is needed but they let you know what that is. Oil light, fuel indicator, wiper levels. Lately cars have started to show woman tendencies, which is not a welcome development. Annoying persistent nagging alarms telling you your seat belt is off or you are about to hit something when you're parking. No one can ever tell a man how to park. Which is how I came to ignore my parking sensors (I mean, what could high tech tell me about judging distance?) and crash into my mother-in-law's car. In my own driveway. The shame. The nasty laughter from my wife and her mum when they came out to see what the sudden crashing noise was. Just me rammed into the crumpled back end of my mother-in-law's car. 'Don't you have rear parking sensors?'

'Fuck you,' I said.

Silently, in my head.

59. THE PREPARATION GENE IN MEN

DIY causes more relationship grief than almost anything else. Most of us don't really like doing it. The dread you get as a bank holiday approaches and you know you have run out of excuses about being too busy to do that flat-pack bookcase or paint the front room. Or finishing that job you started eight months ago when you said you could do the bathroom tiling. And for the last eight months the bathroom has had tiles covering only four square inches. You try and press the point that work cannot possibly continue again until you are allowed to buy some new tools.

If it's not pressure from your partner it's that annoying relative who laughs at your DIY incompetence. 'You do this or Mr Bean?' he says as he spies a wonky shelf.

Men have the preparation gene, or as women see it, the procrastination gene. To us no home improvement can ever be rushed. The pace can be slow but it needs to be. The comedian Bob Mills and I chatted about this once. He got into trouble for wasting time teaching his son how to use the nail gun to shoot balloons. Like any typical man, he saw no inherent danger in this fun activity until his wife came upstairs to the room that was supposed to be being decorated. Bob suggested we need a CD of fake DIY noises. Drilling and banging. This could then cover you reading the paper with a cuppa. Genius.

These makeover shows haven't helped. They make it look easy.

I'm very bad at DIY. My dad just sneers when he comes round to see my latest attempt. Take the children's wardrobe. It said 'Assembly time 20 minutes'. This obviously meant if you had a team of Handy Andys working on it. Two hours and a bottle of wine later, I have somehow, despite some really helpful instructions with no fucking words, just crude drawings of dowels and screws, installed the wardrobe doors upside down. Which means they shut but leave a two-inch gap at the top. My wife noticed this of course and suggested I correct it. We exchanged words and I said actually, just like many great discoveries by accident, it would be handy to have a gap at the top of wardrobe doors so you can see your clothes. My dad did it the next time he was round. Sneering.

Never undertake any DIY project together, unless you enjoy arguing. I remember my wife and I painting the back room together. We started at a different corner. Within 1.7 minutes she had an issue with my brush strokes. Yes, they were grand. I'm sure Michelangelo favoured the broad stroke with paint dripping off the bristles technique. I know something, he didn't have Mrs Fucking Angelo in his ear about the skirting boards getting splashed and seeing bristle hairs on the ceiling. Sure, paint was going on the skirting board but we can sort that all out later, I calmly(ish) said that progress needed to be made. Her speed was too slow (admittedly she was eight months pregnant). Within the hour my wife was 'resting' upstairs in the bedroom with a headache. I did it all myself. I was so proud. She came down and I was looking forward to a begrudging well done. All I heard was 'I don't like the colour' and then I imploded.

60. THE SQUALOR GENE/HAPPY LIVING LIKE A PIG GENE IN MEN

Men left to their own devices are happy to live like pigs. I did a 15-hour radio show and within a few hours I got an email from a woman watching on the studio webcam who said the studio was looking like a minicab office. I looked around, not knowing what on earth she was talking about, to see pizza boxes, empty takeaway cartons and beer cans on the floor. Anyone entering the studio said how badly it smelt. I was happy though.

When my wife came back to mine for the first time she had to make the bed, which hadn't been done for over a week. It actually counts as foreplay I would think.

It's not just that we don't 'see' dirt like women do. It's that our idea of cleaning is very different too. I can hoover and think I have done a pretty impressive job. My wife will then use her microscopic vision to scan the apparently 'cleaned' carpet and point out that I have missed huge areas and start moving bits of furniture that I didn't bother going under. My argument is that no one looks under the settee or coffee table so why worry about making it look clean?

More men are doing housework now. This may have something to do with recent newspaper headlines like this from *The Times*:

IF YOU WANT MORE SEX, DO THE DISHES

This will get any man reaching for the Flash.

Men don't have any problem with mess. Just look at Iraq. Five years ago Bush said, 'Mission Accomplished.'

61. THE SUGGESTIBLE GENE IN MEN

Men are more easily suggestible than women. Many times I have come home with a hideous piece of clothing that I am told I should take back right way. One such time I came home with a shirt that Graham Norton would have considered too gay. The not unattractive lady in the shop had said to me, 'Wow, that shirt really shows off your athletic build.' No one had ever noticed my 'athletic build' before. Why, us breakfast show DJs are famous for it! Of course, the shirt was duly paid for. I remember heading home with the shirt and seeing myself in a new light, imagining myself on the front cover of *Men's Health* magazine with the headline 'GET AN ATHLETIC BUILD LIKE O'CONNELL'S... See inside'. I walked through the front door, carefully so as not to rip it off its hinges with my potent athletic physique. My wife enquired as to what I had purchased. When I showed her she shielded her eyes and couldn't speak, such was its majesty. Several swirling colours and piping. She started giggling when I tried it on and then I played my trump card, which would silence those giggles pretty sharpish. I told her what the woman in the shop had said. The laughing got harder now. Even when she pointed out a thing called commission I still refused to admit I had been duped. When I looked in the mirror I saw what she had seen. A very athletic build. No, my wife was just jealous. It was some time before I found the strength to wear this amazing shirt for the first time. The occasion was my friend Phil's stag night. My wife's howls of derision were nothing compared to the abuse I suffered that night. The best man was in an adult romper suit and I was the one getting all the stick. Someone thought they noticed how it looked in places like moss was growing on the shirt. That was it. 'Moss man' and 'Titchmarsh' became my name for the night. I kept quiet about the athletic build bit.

62. THE CULT GENE IN MEN

It's mainly men who start cults. Isn't it also odd that so many of these cults, run by a man, involve getting closer to God through his underpants.

That nutjob in America who had something like 17 wives. All dressed like the WI at a village fair. Clearly mentally ill. What sane man wants 17 wives?

63. THE SECOND BRAIN GENE IN MEN

Both sexes have brains situated in their craniums but men also have to serve another master. Their second brain. In their pants. Men are often led by their penis. Midlife crisis man shows us that suddenly a man with a loving family will jack it all in for some young floozie at work. His penis is in charge and he is no longer in control of himself. He should really be under house arrest as he's a danger to himself and others.

Socrates said the male libido is 'like being chained to a madman'. He was right. Sadly that madman gets free of the chains sometimes.

A man will tell almost any lie and do all manner of incredibly stupid things to get laid and serve his penis master.

Two recent incidents show this.

WORKER CAUGHT HAVING SEX WITH HENRY HOOVER

MAN CAUGHT HAVING SEX WITH PICNIC TABLE

I could have chosen 'Man who had sex with fence', 'Man who had sex with bicycle', or 'Man arrested for having sex with lamppost'. Let's go back to Henry Hoover.

> The building contractor claimed he was cleaning his underpants with Henry Hoover when he was found naked and on his knees in a hospital's staff canteen.

> A stunned security guard stumbled onto the man in the middle of a compromising act with the cleaner, which has a large smiley face painted on its front and a hose protruding from its 'nose'.

The more I think about it, the more I think that these domestic appliances are leading men astray. Prick teases. 'Large smiley faces.' This man is only human.

When later questioned by his employers, the man said he was vacuuming his underpants, which was 'a common practice in Poland'.

Interesting. I was talking about this story on my radio show and rather than dismiss this excuse through cultural ignorance, I asked any Polish people listening to let me know if this was true. Now, before I go any further I need to tell you I used the word 'pants' during this link. We have people listening all over the world and on this occasion, Poland. I got this great email which is now framed in my toilet at home:

> Christian,
>
> I've been living in Poland since I was born 38 years ago, so I know this for sure. Believe me, the Polish do not hoover cats.
>
> Lots of love from Gdansk, Poland
>
> Marcin

I read this several times before I realised what had happened. Listening to me online through tinny speakers, 'pants' must have sounded like 'pets'. And whether they clean them with hoovers. Though we are still none the wiser about Polish underpant customs, at least I did clear up once and for all that the Polish do not clean cats or any other pets with hoovers.

Let's go back to our man on his hands and knees:

> Henry Hoover is described on a cleaning website as 'famous for its looks, but under its fascia lies a powerful, reliable vacuum cleaner ready to go time and time again'…

> The man is not the first person to be caught in the act with an inanimate object.

> Last year, Robert Stewart was placed on probation for three years after being caught trying to have sex with a bicycle. The 51-year-old was naked from the waist down when two cleaners walked in on him at the Aberley House Hostel in south-west Scotland.

> He paused only to ask, 'What is it, hen?', before continuing to 'move his hips back and forth as if to simulate sex'. The court was told that alcohol was the cause of his problems.

We already knew that though.

Now what about the picnic table shagger? Police were given three DVDs showing the man having sexual intercourse with a picnic table. He admitted to the police that this was true.

What kind of nosy neighbours make not one, not two, but three DVDs of this? We need a 'perverts make the funniest home videos' show. We don't know if he took the table out for dinner first. Did he practise safe sex? Use a condiment? (Sorry.) Could be at risk of splinters. You should have seen the way it was dressed, the tablecloth it had on. It was begging for it.

64. THE DRUNK-DIALLING GENE IN MEN

Most of us men, if honest, have made that ill-advised drunken phone call at 2am a few weeks or months after being dumped. The call goes like this:

You: You bitch, you broke my heart. I furkin' hate you.

Ex: You're such an arsehole.

You: I'd still take you back, you know... Hang on... feeling sick...URRGGGGGH.

Mobiles needs breathalysers that will lock if the user has had over two beers.

65. THE ASKING FOR DIRECTIONS GENE IN WOMEN

A man is never lost.

No man likes asking for directions. Sat Nav has come along and this is the beginning of the end for us. Once our man skills start being replaced by technology the game is up. No, I calm my wife when we are over an hour late, driving through the wrong county, or even country, by saying that we are 'taking the scenic route'.

With rising fuel prices, 'taking the scenic route' is now forcing many men to remortgage the house to fund these fantastical sightseeing adventures.

It was as a kid I first became aware that men never asked for directions. My dad was frequently lost but back then car journeys were more fun as we didn't have to wear seat belts so it was like a fairground ride as you were flung against the car doors/roof/

dashboard. As a treat being allowed to sit in the boot. Constantly asking 'Are we there yet?' as an increasingly demented dad just yelled, 'Shut up or I'm dropping you off at the kids home.'

Women have no problem asking for directions but they have to as their map reading skills are not the best. Firstly they have bent and deformed the actual map. Then it's often the wrong way up. Ellen MacArthur was heralded as a heroine for her circumnavigation of the globe. Truth is she only meant to go to Jersey but misread the map.

66. THE DRESSING-UP GENE IN WOMEN

A woman will go through an intense make-up and hair regime and try several different outfits before picking the right one, just to go to the shops. A man has to be told to put a clean shirt on and no he cannot go to a family get-together in a T-shirt he has had on for the last three days with chilli sauce on.

If we see a woman without make-up we say something like helpful like, 'You OK? You don't look very well.'

67. THE SUPERHERO GENE IN MEN

This may be one of the reasons men are more confident than women. We had Spiderman, Superman and Batman as role models. It may also be why we have problems in relationships.

None of these superheroes were any good with women. Spiderman lived with his auntie and developed great wrist-flicking power like many young single men. Superman was never really a man, as any real man with those powers and strength would not have wanted to keep it a secret. We would have worn a T-shirt with 'I'M SUPERMAN' and used the powers to sleep with women. If a man had the gift of X-ray vision he would immediately use it to look at women, not locate Lex Luther. Batman preferred the company of a young male friend called Robin and wearing tight lycra. Superheroes lived in constant fear of their secret being found out. That they were gay.

For all this, though, they instilled in young boys like me the fantasy that men were strong and invincible. This has not helped us. How many of us have hurt ourselves through stupid physical activities, thinking we were much stronger than we are? I know a friend of mine whose dad was in considerable pain with an ingrown toenail. A short trip to the doctor was all that was required.

However, due to the superhero gene, he simply took his drill to his big toe to relieve some of the pressure. This DIY surgery resulted in a trip to hospital. I gave myself a hernia once when some dick of a yoga instructor told me not to do an exercise called 'wall walking' as I had poor flexibility. I immediately saw this as a challenge. Let me describe this exercise. You stand a metre or so from a wall, facing away from it. You lean back and arch your back, placing the palms of your hands on the wall as if you were Spiderman. You are then supposed to 'walk' down the wall with your hands inch by inch. Maybe a yogi can do this. Not me. But I wouldn't be told. I would show this smug yoga dick my powers. I was doing this when I felt this terrible tearing sensation in me and then a golf-ball-sized bulge appeared in my stomach. It was like *Alien*; something looked like it was trying to get out of me. I never said a thing. Just gingerly walked to the dressing room. Crying. The yoga dick asked me if I was OK. 'Yeah, just gotta shower off...' I didn't say anything to my wife for a few days. Then, fearing it must be penis cancer, I told her.

After I had the hernia operation, which by the way meant I had to have my balls shaved by an old man with shaky hands, I had trouble walking upright for a few days. I went to host the radio show I was doing for 5 Live at that time, 'Fighting Talk', and one of the guests, the legendary Dickie Davies, asked me what was wrong. I told him and like a typical man he one-upped me. He had undergone a double hernia operation and was running within 24 hours. He had shamed me. But then that's why he fronted *World of Sport.* He actually was superhuman. That's why he had that white streak of hair.

68. THE FLOWERS GENE IN MEN

If a man is in a flower shop, two things have happened:

1. He's run out of ideas for a present after six minutes of looking for one.

2. He's fucked up.

I always feel sorry for any man I see working in a flower shop. What can he do? He can't get flowers, that's too easy. Women want to know that you've been inconvenienced in the gift buying. They want to hear, 'I tried 19 different shops before I found it, then it was the wrong size and they had to ring Kuala Lumpaur to get it sent via airmail,' They don't want to know that you spent only one calorie getting it from the local Spar.

I like to surprise my wife with flowers occasionally. Every time I walk through town holding flowers I get two different looks from men and women. From women it's an admiring one. A man getting some lovely flowers for the one he loves, how sweet.

From the men it's always a look saying 'What did you do?'

Quick note: flowers purchased at a garage look they have been purchased at a garage. Women know and any good points you were hoping to get will be lost or worse still deducted.

69. THE 'CAN'T DANCE, SHOULDN'T DANCE' GENE IN MEN

Men can't dance. Their place is at the side of the dance floor getting drunk and laughing at the other guys attempting to dance. Sadly this is no longer acceptable, thanks to TV shows like *Strictly Come Dancing* and *Dancing On Ice*. Darren Gough and Kyran Bracken have hurt mankind. Thanks to their prowess we are now expected to dance. Oh God.

No real man should be dancing.

There are three exceptions to this rule:

Michael Jackson

John Travolta

Patrick Swayze

Those are the only three men on the planet ever to look good on a dance floor. Anyone else is a no no. I mean, look at that light-footed arse Brendan Cole on *Strictly Come Dancing*. There's definitely something wrong with the man. No man should be proud of being able to tell the difference between a foxtrot and a tango. Unless you're big Len Goodman. Notice, though, that Len doesn't actually dance himself. No, he criticises the other idiot men prancing around in leotards.

Reality TV has hurt us bad. Sometimes I feel like Michael Caine in *Zulu*, but instead of heavily armed warriors swarming round my little outpost, it's crappy reality shows, each new one conspiring to take more of my manhood away. Last week ITV and BBC both started shows based on musicals. Primetime on a Saturday night and not a seventies cop show or a cheap Seagal flick in sight. What has the world come to? Look, TV producers, I'm not saying don't make any more shows based on dancing, but at least try and make it a little bit more relevant to me and my brethren.

So to recap, *Dancing On Ice*? NO.

More *Strictly Come Dancing*? NO.

Strictly Come Embarrassing Dad Dancing? YES. With the compulsory Status Quo-off. Now that's entertainment. Come on, Cowell, do your bit for the guys. Call me.

70. THE NICKNAMES GENE IN MEN

I have never once heard my wife pick up the phone and greet the caller with, 'Monkey boy... how are you?'

Men love a nickname, it's in our genes. We seem to have problems with just names. I have worked with men who seemed to be happy addressed as:

Nip Nops

Wanker

G Unit

Milky tits

Fat Phil

Mumbly

71. THE BRIDEZILLA GENE IN WOMEN

This is a gene that only women possess. The gene to actually enjoy planning a wedding. Women know every finite detail of their wedding day from the age of four. Maybe even earlier. Perhaps when they first open their eyes in the delivery room and see the colour of the flowers they think, those won't be at my wedding.

A man will just concern himself with the alcohol situation (the types of beer – to women it's just beer while men know it's a little more complicated than that) and what time to turn up at the church in a clean suit.

It's tradition the man knows nothing of the dress prior to the big day. I wonder who exactly started this 'tradition'? Did this not happen when one day a man being subjected to hour number two of the exact details of the dress have a moment of genius inspiration and say:

'Oh no, I've just realised. I'm not supposed to know any of this until the big day.'

'But I was just about to show you the different shoes that might go nicely with the dress and veil.'

'Love to but could bring us bad luck. Sadly you cannot say another thing about any of this whatsoever. Oh, and I cannot see you the night before either. Have to stay with my best man – no choice.'

It had to be a guy. Using women's genetic fear of 'bad luck' and other weird juju.

Result!

72. THE DREAMS ARE INTERESTING GENE IN WOMEN

No, they're not.

73. THE LOOSE CHANGE GENE IN MEN

I seem to somehow accumulate lots of loose change. Yet due to the presence of the mighty loose change gene, I will always pay with a crisp note rather than bother to try and find the exact change.

I fear being one of those people that the rest of the queue stare at and hate. You're at the till fumbling with your coinage, bits of tissues coming out your pockets that have been through the wash and are now solidified. It's just not manly. Notes are for men.

Sure, change weighs us down but maybe that's why men don't suffer so much with weight gain as women. It's a workout regime just carrying kilos of coins around like a bus conductor. Add in the calories burnt fiddling with it. Rarely do women have pockets full of coins. The reason of course is that they pay their EXACT share of the bill.

74. THE LATE NIGHT DRUNK COOKING GENE IN MEN

You have had a few cold ones. You have had too many cold ones. You enjoy a hearty Indian or Chinese meal at a restaurant. You arrive home having had your fill of food and beer. The time is 1am.

Do you:

a) Retire to bed.

b) Immediately start opening cupboards noisily, heat up a frying pan and begin cooking. Drunk.

The answer is of course b). What is commonly known as the ready steady drunk gene.

I said earlier that mobile phones should have breathalysers fitted to stop guys drink-dialling. I'm also going to suggest kitchen utensils and ovens have them too.

75. THE NEAR TO, ON TOP, NEXT TO GENE IN MEN

My wife discovered this gene in me. For some unknown reason, I have trouble, almost to the point of aversion, putting things where they really should be.

Clothes will be placed near to, on top, next to, but not IN the dirty clothes basket. Same with dirty plates – near to, on top of and next to the dishwasher, but rarely in. Lacking the ability to see things through. This is why many of us die before women. We cannot finish any job properly. Even life.

76. THE WANDERING GENE IN MEN

This is the gene that annoys my wife more than almost anything else I do. We'll go to the supermarket together, and then I will wander off to get something and get lost. Losing myself and my wife. I then start looking down aisles trying to remember what my wife was wearing, and indeed what she looks like. What she really gets annoyed about is when I just wander off without telling her. I do this all the time.

She will be dawdling somewhere, taking her time, examining things like women like to do and I will just... drift away like a child's balloon.

Many of us get lost while out shopping together. If it's not because I have wandered off then it's due to the incredible speed my wife is capable of. Suddenly she can, without any warning, fire up some unseen motor engine that I cannot keep up with. It's not running. It's not walking. It's something in between. It scares me.

77. THE CRAP GIFTS GENE IN MEN

No, I still don't know what possessed me to get her a foot spa. She said it was something you got your nan. I said that's because they appreciate relaxed feet and you will too with this great gift. I remember even giving a demonstration of its majesty like you see on the shopping channels. You could be watching your favourite TV show while luxuriating in the foot spa – heaven!

Men are genetically programmed to purchase crap gifts. It's either totally wrong or the wrong shape/size/colour. How many times have you found yourself pathetically protesting, 'The women in the shop said you'd really love it.'

Brian from my radio show did something really dumb, even for him. He gave his mum a book for Mother's Day. What's the problem in that? you may think. It was the exact same one he gave her for Christmas.

The timing of buying the gifts matters to women as well. I remember two days before my wife's birthday saying to her, thinking it would get me some kudos, 'Someone's going birthday shopping today,' and her getting quite upset as I hadn't got her anything already. 'But it's not until two days' time. As long as you get something who cares when I buy it?' was my watertight defence, or so I thought. Apparently it is not the thought that counts. It's the time, blood, sweat and tears you put into finding the gift that counts.

78. THE NAMING THINGS THAT SHOULDN'T HAVE NAMES GENE IN WOMEN

Bessie

Hoopty

Lollipop

Tilly

Jelly Bean

No, these aren't the names that Chris Martin and Gwyneth didn't use when naming their kid Apple. These are the names that some women I know (who seem perfectly sane and reasonable) have named THEIR CARS. Yes, NAMED THEIR CARS.

Why would you name a car? Why? Sure, men love their cars, which is itself a gene, but we still wouldn't name them. Although we might talk about them as a 'he' or 'she'- that's acceptable.

With women, it doesn't stop at cars you know. Other inanimate objects get named too. Women even like to give us men a name. 'Pookie' or 'Snugglekins'. In the bedroom, fine. Outside of it, never. Once you accept it, they never respect you again. You are Pookie.

Phew. That's all the 78 genetic differences. This has never been attempted before and its impact will be up there with Stephen Hawking's *Brief History of Time*. History will remember me for this pioneering work.

I'm ready for my Nobel Peace Prize now.

VI

MEN AND EMOTIONS

THE MADNESS THAT LURKS WITHIN ALL MEN...

It's a commonly held belief among men that women are more emotional than men. More emotionally complicated. Just a quick flick through my wife's magazines – how to be a better mate, how to keep your man happy at home and in bed, how to lose pounds, must-have shoes – leaves me feeling overwhelmed. So many articles on things called 'feelings'. In contrast, men's magazines show lots of women half naked. With some articles on cars chucked in, how to get 'rock-hard abs' and poncey man bags costing £5,000.

I think the truth is that both men and women are emotional. Just look at Kevin Keegan. Women are more emotionally complicated and are born that way. That's why they do things like pluck their eyebrows then draw them back on with a crayon. But men – men are capable of far greater madness. For years we've thought women are the nuts ones but now I'm not so sure.

Fatal Attraction gave us the 'bunny boiler' with Glenn Close teaching us never to have affairs and own small furry pets. Alanis Morissette still scares us with 'You Oughta Know', her hit about being dumped by her boyfriend despite fellating him at the theatre. Maybe she just wanted a kiss afterwards and that's when it went bad. It's become a bunny boilers anthem. Surely no man could write lyrics like Morissette's:

> *I want you to know, that I'm happy for you*
> *I wish nothing but the best for you both*

Yeah right. Whether you're a man or a woman, you only want to hear that since your break-up their life has turned to shit and they sit around in their pants all day watching *Trisha* and crying, eating Cheerios without milk.

> *An older version of me*
> *Is she perverted like me*
> *Would she go down on you in a theatre*

Well, it's a question I guess many men have at the back of their minds on a first date, but it's picking the right moment to ask, isn't it? Perhaps it should be a question on dating websites:

Age:

Hobbies:

One final question. Would you go down on me in a theatre?

Note how it's a 'theatre' where the act is performed. Theatres are a bit boring for men, aren't they? It's one way to encourage attendance, I guess. 'Free blow job for every guy.' Be sold out for years. Back to Alanis:

> *Does she speak eloquently?*

It's very hard to if you're doing *that* in a theatre.

> *You seem very well, things look peaceful*
> *I'm not quite as well, I thought you should know*
> *Did you forget about me Mr Duplicity*
> *I hate to bug you in the middle of dinner*

Oh God, she's rocked up at Nando's while he's having some peri-peri chicken with the new Miss Duplicity. Just before the theatre.

> *It was a slap in the face how quickly I was replaced*
> *Are you thinking of me when you fuck her*

You're swearing now and causing a scene, Alanis. Someone call security... Calm down... People are looking round... Fancy coming to the theatre with us?

> *And every time I scratch my nails down someone else's back*
> *I hope you feel it... well can you feel it*

I just thought it was a spot but now you mention it... Look, email me, let's keep in touch.

You, you, you oughta know

You're scaring me now.

Without doubt one of the best and scariest break-up songs ever. And it's written by a woman. Could a man have written it? Both sexes handle break-ups badly – it's a universal life theme, heartbreak. I don't think you're really a man until you have had your heart broken, put in a blender and then made to drink it. (*See also* Rites of Passage.)

TOP FIVE BREAK-UP SONGS

They would take away my DJ card if I didn't have my top five break-up songs:

1. 'DON'T THINK TWICE, IT'S ALRIGHT' BY BOB DYLAN

When I hit 30 I started to appreciate Dylan, having spent the previous 30 years hating him. Maybe it's a sign I'm getting more mature, or my hearing's going. His break-up album masterpiece *Blood on the Tracks* is a must-have but I've put this in from *The Freewheelin' Bob Dylan*.

2. 'GO YOUR OWN WAY' BY FLEETWOOD MAC

Lindsey Buckingham should be something of a hero for men. It's one thing to tell your ex that she's a selfish cow, but then to get her to sing along with it. Now that's some man!

3. 'I HOPE YOU'RE HAPPY NOW' BY ELVIS COSTELLO

What a brilliantly bitter song. Bonus points for having the words 'pork sword' in it.

4. 'SONG FOR THE DUMPED' BY BEN FOLDS FIVE

Short and to the point.

So you wanted to take a break
Slow it down some and have some space
Well fuck you too!

Ends like many relationship break-ups, asking for outstanding money owed and clothes back. Genius. There are only a few occasions when I have broken the host-subject protocol and asked someone I'm interviewing to sign something. You never saw Parkinson lean over and ask David Niven or Muhammad Ali to 'sign something for me or me mates won't believe I've actually met you'. Ben was one and oddly enough the other was Elvis Costello. Must be something about the authors of bitter-sweet break-up songs. Oh, and Chuck 'The Iceman' Liddell, former UFC Light Heavyweight champ. I don't know if Chuck has penned a break-up song. Maybe we all have one in us.

5. 'DRY YOUR EYES MATE' BY THE STREETS

A genuine heartbreaker by the bard of the streets. Always gets me. It's a true modern classic love song. Forget about him looking like the kind of person you would cross the road to avoid. He captures the whole run of emotions we go through when it's over. Even the overworn man-to-dumped-man classic 'there's plenty more fish in the sea' works.

6. BONUS TRACK

I know it's a Top Five but a very special entry must be 'Ruby Don't Take Your Love To Town' by Kenny Rogers. Poor Kenny, he's a Vietnam vet in a wheelchair watching his missus get tarted up to go out and 'take her love to town' . YOU BITCH. My words, not

Kenny's. My eldest daughter is called Ruby and I made a little CD for her when she came home from the hospital after being born. This song was on it and suddenly it became horribly inappropriate. My wife shot me a look when Kenny starts wishing he had a gun to put her 'in the ground'.

Early exposure to TV detective Jim Rockford taught me that there is no shame in running away from potentially threatening situations. However, this may be part of the problem of how we struggle with our emotions sometimes. Women's emotions are like insurgents, ready to ambush you at any moment. Men are like unexploded grenades. They can just go off. With no warning; just go nuts.

Maybe there is a 'dickhead DNA' – 'dDNA' as it will be referred to from now on – in us and at some point it can be activated by as yet unknown powers. Maybe it's set during all those nocturnal erections we get. I think the penis, unknown to us, acts as a kind of antenna receiving new instructions from our overlords, possibly monkeys. Like that big thing sticking out of a dodgem, getting the juice. Same with those night-time erections. I could be on to something here. How many times have we suspected we are really ruled by what Billy Connolly calls 'the hairy brain'? Let me ask this question. Is it that our balls and penis are on the outside of us, or are we on the outside of them?

What is it with men that makes us so odd at times? You have to be honest; we are just as mad as women. They may be born that way but when we suddenly go bad it's really bad. The dDNA forces otherwise decent and good men to grow pony tails, wear leather pants and run off with one of the Cheeky Girls. Or tell the world they have bulimia like John Prescott. Former Deputy PM and much missed, if you ask me, Prezza said he could 'sup a whole tin of condensed milk', eat trifles 'for ever' and chomp his way through a Chinese restaurant's entire menu. At first I misread this and thought he could eat an entire Chinese restaurant. Then 15 minutes later feel hungry and do the same thing again. We all laughed at a big man saying he had this illness – mainly because bulimics don't usually weigh 23 tons and have to be transported in two separate Jaguars. One for each thigh. Maybe he meant he was beerlimic, a condition many men suffer from which should never be laughed at.

CANOE MAN

Prezza blamed stress. Stress and men is a fatal combination. Like poor old Arthur Fowler and the Christmas Club money in *EastEnders*. But the single greatest recent example of the phenomenon 'Nuts Man' is Canoe Man. Not Canoe Woman or Canoe Lady. Oh no. Canoe Man.

We're all familiar with the story. A man disappears after a tragic canoe accident, his family mourn his death. Some years later he reappears, claiming to not know what happened. A similar thing happened to Harold Bishop in *Neighbours*. Harold was swept away by a freak wave, feared dead. Then five years later Helen Daniels found him alive and well working for the Salvation Army under the name 'Ted'. He did the right thing and went back to Madge. What I'm saying is if it can happen to Harold Bishop, then... maybe this is where Canoe Man got the idea.

Let's go back to the story.

CANOE MAN PART 2

A grown-up man, an adult, suddenly hatches the plan to disappear, fake his own death in a bizarre canoe accident and get the insurance money. Let's just stop a moment here for some quiet reflection. If I was going to fake my own death, a canoe mishap wouldn't even make it onto the shortlist. Surely as a man you want to be remembered as a hero? Women getting misty-eyed at the mere mention of your name. Men wishing they had an ounce of your selfless bravery. My possible fake deaths would have been:

- A house fire saving some orphans and a dog. At least 20 of each.

- Taking a bullet for Jeff Stelling and Des Lynam.

- Saving the country by flying a nuclear bomb into Sharon Osbourne.

- Running over the *Sex and the City* girls in the tin bath used every episode in *Last of the Summer Wine*.

But wait. This guy's a smart bloke. Like all men he's a master of thinking things through. He then reappears at his poor wife's back door a year later. Tapping on the window by the bins, I'd imagine. I mean, he couldn't just knock on the front door, could he, shouting through the letter box? 'Coo-ee, guess who it is?' No. That would be plain stupid. Did he have some flowers to help ease this reunion? Her favourite chocolates? 'Sorry, they'd run out of Cadbury's Sensations, got you some Heroes instead.'

After what we can only guess was a pretty spirited chat – 'You're getting carried away now, darling, calm down, put the kettle on. Look, I got you some flowers...' – he then moves in with her. While still technically dead. And lives next door in a bedsit from where he can nip in to see his wife for some hot loving via a hole in the wall and the back of the wardrobe. Simple. And we think women are nuts. This is what men do. We are ideas people. Trouble is, part of me is thinking this might be the perfect relationship. Can't be told off for not folding the hand towels correctly if you're dead, can you? Not expected to have an opinion of curtain colours if you're not actually alive. Has his wicked way then goes back to his bed via a hole in the back of a wardrobe. This guy's a genius!

It gets better, though. While living this lie he obviously has to be extremely careful when wandering around his neighbourhood in case he is recognised. So he walks among us in disguise. And what a disguise! A walking stick and a fake limp. Sorry, I forgot the cap. Fuck me. Hardly Jack Bauer, is he?

'Isn't that old Bob who died in that bizarre canoe mishap?'

'No, it can't be. That guy has a limp and a walking stick. Bob didn't.'

'Oh yeah.'

I mean, not even a fake beard like the late Beadle. Just a walking stick and limp. Probably from a joke shop for under a fiver.

Men are capable of great and terrifying acts of madness. In the news recently was a story about two men whose flatmate died.

A sad passing. Time for some mournful reflection about the fragility of our existence. That and time to put him in a wheelbarrow and try and collect his social security cheque. No, this really happened.

I can hear the giggling now as the pensioners – sorry, did I not mention they were over 60? – loaded their mate into the wheelbarrow, no doubt saying, 'It's what he would have wanted.'

This DNA which suddenly goes off in a man and turns him into some kind of wide-eyed loon can also help him achieve greatness. Like Kent Couch.

KENT COUCH

A real man of genius. This guy is why the world needs us. Kent put 105 helium balloons on his chair and flew. Yeah, just let that sink in. Took off, in a garden chair!

Took off into the atmosphere and flew, from the comfort of his garden chair. Who the hell isn't impressed with that? As we know, all men hate moving from their seat once they've occupied it. Most of us would have no problem if society made it permissible to soil ourselves rather than leave 24 at a key moment for an annoying toilet trip. Or to get the phone. Or to leave the house in the event of a fire. Science took a major leap forward in my mind when I read the other day that we will soon have self-cleaning pants. This is big news for men. We could get away with wearing the same pair of pants from 1 January to 31 December.

Kent Couch, I love you. Let me tell you more about this genius.

It's the summer of 2007, and our man – hero, really – settles into his lawn chair with some important provisions, his snacks. I would guess that is the most important part of preparing for any journey into the skies on a helium-balloon-powered chair, your snacks. Whether watching a movie, the big match or *X Factor*, your choice of snacks is vital. One false Dorito and... well, it's not worth thinking about. Back in the bloody kitchen looking for new selections, wasting valuable arse-sitting TV time.

Anyway, his snacks selected, he adds the less important things. Parachute and 105 large helium balloons. I would imagine he did what any sane grown-up man would do and used the helium to get a squeaky funny voice first.

- Garden Chair... Check.

- Snacks... Check.

- Parachute... Check.

- 105 Large Helium Balloons... Check.

He checks his instruments, which will measure his speed and altitude, and the gallons of water that will act as ballast, and then heads off, and up, into the Oregon sky heading via his GPS to Idaho. Brilliant. Apart from the GPS bit. We all know those things are devil tools. Any man using them is adding to our own redundancy in society. We're hurting ourselves, men.

Kent made 193 miles in nine hours in his chair, not all the way to Idaho but nonetheless a remarkable and worthwhile trip. It should have attracted greater attention around the world. When the space shuttle took off for its maiden voyage, we stopped our school lessons for a special assembly to watch it all. The same should have been done for Kent's voyage. Kids would have been shown a prime example of why men are important. Pioneers. With snacks and flying garden chairs.

This has to be the future of air travel for us. From our own garden chairs. No more check-in queues at those hugely irritating RAPID BAG DROPS which mean the exact opposite. Or having shampoo taken away from us in case you storm the cockpit with some Herbal Essences.

Kent followed the trail-blazing path laid down by another aeronautical genius, Larry Walters (more kids need to be named Larry and Kent, enough of Jack and Harry), in 1982, who managed to rise three miles about Los Angeles in a chair lifted by balloons. Larry scared the hell out of an airline pilot who had to radio the control tower that he had just passed a 'guy in a lawn chair'.

Try that now without telling the relevant authorities and you'd be gunned down by scrambled jets! Flown by Jack Bauer. 'Goddamnit, Chloe, those terrorist bastards have got balloon chairs... get me the the president. Now, Chloe, goddamnit!'

All of us need a dream. Luther King. Kent Couch.

So, yes, women can occasionally boil the odd rabbit but men have no problem living in wardrobes.

MEN AND SHOWING EMOTION TO EACH OTHER

Crying is a taboo for men. I have shared hugs and tears with many men, complete strangers, at sports events, sober or drunk. My wife came running up to me when she saw me sitting on the couch one morning with tears streaming down my face. 'Oh God, what's happened?' she said breathlessly as I moved my head to get a better view of Matthew Pinsent getting another gold medal on the TV screen. (Even that medal for the curling got me going.) Did I shy away from those tears like a dog caught eating his own sick? No, I wore those tears like a hot, salty, wet badge of honour. (All right, I did try passing it all off as a rare allergic reaction to eating too many Doritos in my own couch Olympics.) Even the greatest Bond ever, Sean Connery, has admitted to being reduced to tears by athletics.

At any sporting event, hugs, tears and beers are all fine. Take away the sporting context and suddenly you're a big girl. I remember going to see Clint Eastwood's fine movie *Million Dollar Baby* with my wife. I also remember her saying to me five minutes into the film through snarled teeth, 'You never said it was a boxing movie!' I also forgot to mention the storyline was about euthanasia. It's not really a date movie, is it? Richard Curtis is yet to tackle the rom-com pillars of boxing and mercy killing with Hugh Grant and Colin Firth. He will, though, I'm sure.

After watching *Million Dollar Baby* I was blubbing big snotty man tears so badly I couldn't drive home and was slurring like a punch-drunk boxer myself. Don't laugh. Your disdain for me is nothing compared to my wife's. Women say they want a sensitive man but they don't really. No one knows what to do with a crying man. Remember Gazza at the 1990 World Cup? Gary Lineker signalled to the bench for help.

I regard men who cry openly as weak and yet I cry very easily these days. It might be since becoming a dad. *The West Wing* has had me in tears more than anything in my life. I was there at the joyous occasions of my children's births but it was so awe-inspiring I didn't actually cry. (Or it could have been that I was busy thinking about boys coming to take them out in 18 years time, then remembering what I was like at that age and thinking I may try and bring them up gay. Which is why they are listening to a constant loop of k.d. lang right now and playing with My Little Power Tools.)

Men fear tears because it shows we are not in control of our emotions and this to us is what women do. Lose control of their emotions.

I saw a Top Ten of movies men cry at recently and I wasn't surprised to see that seven of the ten were sports films. Sport is our get out of jail free card for men and tears.

There are certain films where no man should feel any shame in letting the tears flow. I'm sure many of us were moved to tears in *Animal House* when the campus cops were removing everything from Delta House, even the stuff they never stole. *Titanic* made me cry but that was because the person I took to the cinema never put out.

MY TOP FIVE MAN TEARS MOVIES

In no particular order, hankies at the ready...

1. FIELD OF DREAMS

Kevin Costner stars in this guaranteed tear-jerker for men. He's a farmer, Ray, who hears voices telling him 'if you build it, he will come'. Similar thing happened to me but it was my wife's voice about some flat-pack that needed doing.

The tears come when he starts playing catch with his dead dad. I loved playing catch with my dad. Add the movie catnips for men of nostalgia, time travel and sport, and hey presto, you have an instant man flick. The ghosts of former baseball legends start turning up. It's a Derek Acorah wet dream.

Now I'm not saying all of this movie holds up over time. His wife Annie just letting her husband build a baseball diamond in the back garden because 'some voices' told him to is unrealistic. In real life Ray would have got a curt 'Over my fucking dead body' or 'Have you been drinking?'

It's left to his brother-in-law to tell him to knock it all on the head or he will go bankrupt. (The hard-hearted brother-in-law is a staple in many man movies.) The whole DIY project, like so many men undertake, seems doomed until James Earl Jones turns up. Here it's also a little unbelievable as at no point does Ray ask James Earl Jones to 'do his Darth Vader voice'.

It made me think about building a football pitch in my garden for former Southampton legends like Mickey Channon, Keegan and

Le Tissier to come and play on, but the kids want a swing there and we've got a mole problem.

The last 15 minutes are all you need to see to start the man tears and I have contacted the Home Office with an idea that they beam this last bit around troublesome inner-city areas. The hoodies will watch, learn, cry and down cheap mixer drinks. Then start breaking windows playing catch with ghosts.

Psychologist David Powell said in an article in *Reader's Digest*: 'There's a 95 per cent tear factor when a group of men watch *Field of Dreams*... Sports is the archetypal bond between men and their fathers, and for most men the most primitive, important relationship in their lives is with their dads.'

If you are not crying you must be dead. Or maybe never played catch with a ghost dad.

2. ROCKY IV

A masterpiece. Dolph Lundgren's Ivan Drago has a punch of '2000 PSI', and anyone who has filled their car tyres knows this is something to fear. The damage that could do to small inflatables isn't worth thinking about. With this atomic power he pummels Rocky for 15 rounds when Apollo died after just two, despite being bigger than Rocky.

Not only winning but also making a poignant speech. (Or asking where the loos are. It's hard to tell with Stallone sometimes.)

This movie single-handedly brought down the USSR. They simply couldn't handle its powerful message. They saw it and the game was up.

The tears are over Rocky's former adversary and now bestest mate Apollo Creed's death. Rocky is beside himself at his death: we know this through the use of montages of the two of them running in slow motion on a beach, which all men love to do. And what better way to also reflect on a good friend's death than driving around listening to a cheesy eighties pop song.

Ivan Drago is clearly on various steroids, his gonads virtually glowing in some scenes.

Rocky also somehow got the perfect beach tan despite training in the Siberian snow. I loved the fact they had measured Drago's strength and it was, I quote, that of a 'great white shark'. Have they measured the strength of a great white shark and found it to be that of 'Ivan Drago, you know, the Russian who killed Apollo'?

It's a tear-jerker. Who can watch when Ivan Drago clubs Apollo to death with the strains of James Brown playing in the background without crying? The Oscar Academy should hang their heads in shame for not giving it Best Picture in 1985.

We saw Rocky start his day running up a mountain shouting his opponent's name. He doesn't appear to shave unless his wife is around. Actually I know that many of us, when wives and girlfriends are away, relish the chance to dress and look slovenly, experimenting with facial hair like goatees. Rocky is no different. He grows a beard to show us he no longer cares about things like shaving, as he must fight the man who killed his mate. He even screws up a picture of Drago as beardy Rocky. Shaved Rocky may not have done this. Beardy Rocky sometimes looks like a folk singer with huge biceps.

After defeating Drago and communism, Rocky returns home to find out his son has mysteriously aged ten years. I feared the worst when I first heard *Rocky VI* was in production, thinking the old slugger would be fighting prostate cancer and wondering where he left his car keys and chasing those pesky kids off his front lawn. But it was good. A better way to end the series than the shocking *Rocky V*.

When I interviewed Mr T, who played Clubber Lang, I told him of my tears over Creed's death. He wasn't impressed and even went so far as to say it was Apollo's own fault that he died as no man should 'bring dancing and the like to a fight'.

3. THE SHAWSHANK REDEMPTION

In many prison movies and TV shows, the wardens or governor of the prison usually hate doing their tax returns and sure could do with a smart inmate to help. Same here with this great movie about two innocent inmates who bond and one of them may have to bite a man's penis. Without any ketchup.

After watching this you learn that if you ever are banged up and need to store something, put it behind a poster. That and playing some classical music loudly will make everyone stop what they are doing and look up to the sky.

The best job in prison is always wheeling the books around in the library. It must be heavily over-subscribed with a waiting list. All that said, the final scene with the boat on the beach (I'm no boat expert but is that the best place to build a boat, right by the shore?) is brilliant. Morgan Freeman is great and seems to be part Irish as he has freckles in some scenes.

That beer must have tasted great.

4. THE GODFATHER

Not only one of the greatest movies ever made but also has some of the great scenes in movie history for men. Almost put me off oranges for life. And fishing.

The tear-jerker scenes are of course the death Don Vito Corleone, who dies playing with his grandson in the garden. He survives an assassination attempt but is killed by a heart attack brought on by shoving too many marshmallows in his mouth.

The other is when Michael gives Fredo the 'kiss of death' after finding out about his brother's betrayal.

I cried again at *The Godfather: Part III* but that was about what they had done to these great movies with that crap.

5. TOP GUN

Sure Goose's death isn't cinema's most heroic. Not in a hail of bullets or taking one for his partner. No, poor Goose bangs his head on the roof of the F-14.

An inquiry clears Maverick but he is so overwhelmed with guilt he blows out his girlfriend Kelly McGillis and goes on long rides on his motorbike.

Later on in active combat he gets stuck in the jet wash, just like what happened when Goose lost his life. He loses his nerve, fearing he might bang his head and die. Clutching Goose's dog tags, Mav asks his mate to speak to him one last time. It's almost too much to watch.

He finds strength and gets back into the dogfight, taking down three Migs and covering Iceman. Iceman tells Maverick 'he can be his wingman anytime'. There can be no greater compliment from a man with great teeth and hair who seems to fancy the arse off you.

Maverick finally lets go of Goose's tags and drops them into the ocean. I mean, it might have been nicer to give them to Goose's son. Or put them on eBay.

A special mention should also go to *Rudy.* Not that well known over here but do yourself a favour and watch it. Yes, it's about American football but if you played sport or more importantly like me were rejected for the school football team on the grounds you were utter shit, you'll be crying at this.

The film's based on the true story of short-arse Daniel 'Rudy' Ruttiger and his dream of playing football at Notre Dame University. Only thing is he's a bit thick and half the size of the other kids. Which is why he's played by a hobbit (Sean Astin, Sam in *Lord of the Rings*).

He forgets his silly dream and goes to work with his old man at the steelworks. Then his best mate Pete is killed and this makes Rudy decide to quit and follow his dream. Any ideas what happens next?

I won't ruin it for you but the man tears will come. It's got the triumph of a hobbit over those who told him he would never amount to anything, camaraderie, the cheesiest but teariest

ending ever, and locker-room speeches that Churchill would have
been proud of.

EMOTIONAL TV

Television has created some classic tear-jerking moments for
men too. Leo dying in *The West Wing* is one. *The West Wing*
is the very best kind of fantasy TV. It's the people you wished
were running America and therefore the world. I remember
sinking a few beers one lunchtime with David Tennant and we
started arguing about the top five greatest TV shows ever. This
show was one we both agreed on, admitting it actually had us in
tears more than any other TV show. We then started kissing and
exploded in a moment of unbridled gayness.

Then there was Bobby Jr getting shot in *The Sopranos*. TV was
made for *The Sopranos*. It may never get any better (though *The
Wire* is damn close). I read that even genuine Mafioso like and
approve of *The Sopranos*, although one wrote to the show's creator
David Chase saying that the barbecue scene at Tony's was
unrealistic. No Mafia don would ever wear shorts.

I also fought back the man tears in *Dr Who* when Rose left to
become a whore on ITV. And what about that incredible final
scene of *Blackadder Goes Forth*?

One of the most memorable TV moments for me is Chris Eubank
proposing to his girlfriend, smeared in the blood of his opponent
Nigel Benn. Eubank had just become the World Middleweight
Champion in 1990, back when British boxing was some of the
world's most exciting. ITV's Gary Newbon was conducting the

post-fight chat with Eubank live to the nation when he suddenly proposed to his girlfriend Karen.

' ...I told you I could do it, Karen. Well, maybe I didn't, but I always thought I would. My chin is cast-iron... Karen, can we get married now? Marry me, Karen.'

What could have been more emotional or romantic? How could she have said no to any suitor who had a 'cast-iron' chin? Seconds later the whole thing got even better when Eubank asked Newbon if he could 'go to hospital now'.

There is a sad note, however, because Eubank divorced recently. As always we can rely on Chris Eubank for an articulate explanation. He blamed his hijacking of a beer lorry that was blocking the road, which got him a £450 fine.

'It was the straw that broke Karen's back. If I see something wrong I will act. I have a superhero complex. That's what ruined my marriage.'

One TV show I have to limit my exposure to is *Extreme Makeover: Home Edition*. If you haven't seen or heard of it before it's a makeover show which is OK for men to watch. You cannot watch them back to back or you would drown in your own tears. I'm serious. People contact the show who have just the worst lives. A man with a silly name, Ty, and a design team rebuild their home in seven days, complete with the finest finishes. Then they have the big reveal. That's the moment you start the man tears in the most undignified way.

Sex and the City makes me cry too. Because it's evil.

VII

HOLLYWOOD: THE MALE MORAL COMPASS

Like most people I often find myself in situations where I am struggling in a moral quagmire. There have been many times when I've been genuinely confused about which path to take in life. As we all know, you can't really turn to friends for advice. Talk about football, make fun of each other and get drunk together, yes. Advice sessions? No. What about family and relatives? Nope. Christmas and Easter is enough, thank you very much. Wife? As much as I love her and trust her judgement implicitly, the line between advice and nagging is far too blurred for my liking. Instead I use an amazing resource for my moral compass. When looking for the perfect template of man, you can't get much better than Hollywood.

The film industry has a history of creating men who we can identify with. Got a man problem? Then I'm certain a strong male character from a famous film can give you advice. For instance, you're in two minds whether or not to buy a new car. Pop *Bullit* in the DVD player. Half an hour of Steve McQueen chasing wrong-uns up and down the streets of San Francisco will soon convince you that your Nissan Micra just isn't the way to go. Want some tips on picking up the ladies? Let Sir Michael Caine in *Alfie* throw you a bone. However, pick the films you take advice from very carefully. I don't want any of you getting the wrong idea when you watch *Last Tango in Paris*. Butter is for putting on bread and cooking with. AND NOTHING ELSE.

Another great example of how we are influenced by film is the ease with which we can quote from them. We often forget things like birthdays, anniversaries and turning the hob off, but ask us what colour Mini Michael Caine rides in at the end of *The Italian Job* or to recite the last line of *Goodfellas* and it's total recall. (It's blue and 'I'm a nobody, I get to live the rest of my live like a schnook' in case you thought I was bluffing.) For some reason, movies connect with the male psyche like no other phenomenon. I know that people complain about the dumbing down of *Mastermind* but I bet I could win the fucker if they let me have 'The wisecracks of Steven Seagal in his films from 1988 to 1995' as my specialist subject.

When DCI Gene Hunt roared onto our screens, something very special happened. Men had a real balls-out, arse-kicking, un-PC hero. Policemen put his poster up in their stations. Actor Philip Glenister told me that once, being driven home from a day's filming, he was pulled over by the actual police. After a few minutes quizzing his driver, Philip, in full Gene mode, wound down his window and said, 'What the fuck are you doing, son? You should be catching nonces not hassling us.'

The cop did a double take and said, 'Oh, it's you, sorry, on you go.'

The huge love for the Gene Genie showed me that we care a lot about our male heroes on TV and in films. From Tony Soprano to James Bond. They really matter to us. But they have also changed to reflect men's changing role is society. Bond no longer screws everything in sight. Our heroes became PC and watered down. Gene Hunt was the antidote to that and that's why we love him.

Who are the important men that we really respect and admire?

Let's go to the movies first.

THE BUDDY MOVIE

Of course the male film-making in its purest form is the buddy movie. It's always two guys thrown together in unlikely circumstances (usually cops but not always), forced to work together and become friends by the end of the movie. The legendary movie critic calls them 'Wunza' movies. As in 'wunza crazy loose cannon and wunza play by the rules kinda guy'. It's from these movies we can learn the most about being men.

MY TOP TEN GUY MOVIES

Let me just say that this list went through many incarnations and was very hard to whittle down to ten. Some of you will agree with me, some of you will disagree with me and some of you will be just plain confused. I conducted an extensive survey of the population, spent hours of research in libraries and polled the finest male minds of our age. OK, that's a lie. I got horribly drunk and had a good old nosey through IMDb. I woke up the next morning with ten films scrawled on the back of a Chinese takeaway menu. Here they are in no particular order:

10 Kung Po Chilli Chicken... £4.95

Hang on, that really is number ten on the list...

Let me start again.

10. DUMB AND DUMBER

One of the great comedy movies of the modern age. The roles of the two main characters defy the age-old tradition of the funny and straight man – these are two funny men, Harry and Lloyd, on a mission to hand back a lost suitcase to a girl simply because Lloyd has a crush on her. Along the way they make a fortune, lose a fortune, fall in love and take on the mob. But none of that really matters because *Dumb and Dumber* is the purest form of what makes men go to the movies. Really puerile stuff that shouldn't make you laugh but does. Things like two men smacking each other across the arse with canes; a whole scene devoted to Jeff Daniels emptying his guts into a broken toilet. *Dumb and Dumber* is an amazing film and perfect for men because it doesn't worry too much about the plot. It's too busy cramming in as many jokes as possible. It has possibly the highest gags per minute ratio of any film since *Airplane!*. If an alien were to come down to earth, you wouldn't show him *Citizen Kane*, you'd show him something that had galactic appeal. Two men tricking another man into drinking a bottle of urine. It's full of physical comedy that anybody can understand.

Things men learn from *Dumb and Dumber*:

- It's better to cram in as many gags as possible rather than worry about stuff like the plot.

- 'We've landed on the moon' may be the funniest thing Carrey ever says in his career.

- Your life hits an all-time low when your pets' heads are falling off.

- Who doesn't want to hear the most annoying sound in the world?

- John Denver is full of crap.

9. TOP GUN

No man dislikes the film *Top Gun*. If any man claims not to like it, then look down his pants and check he has the right genitalia because *Top Gun* is a male institution. It has one of the greatest love stories in cinema. I know what you're thinking: is Tom Cruise and Kelly McGillis really the greatest love story on film? But I'm actually talking about Goose and Maverick. I defy any man not to cry when Maverick is cradling Goose's head in the sea. I don't quite believe that *Top Gun* is a movie with a homosexual subtext but I firmly believe that it celebrates the best thing about being a man and the bond between us that can never be broken, not even by a heat-seeking missile. It says that if men want to hang out and fly planes, then that's OK. If they want to hang round in locker rooms wearing hand towels then that's OK. If they want to go down to the beach and oil each other up and play topless volleyball against each other, then that's er... OK? The point I'm trying to get across is that sometimes a film needs to revel in masculinity and *Top Gun* does all that and more.

It turns the mundane into the spectacular. The main hero, played by a young Tom Cruise, is called Pete Mitchell. But in this film they all have 'call signs' so Pete becomes 'Maverick'. That's another reason why we love this film so much – we all love nicknames. All men dream of having call signs in real life. Imagine ringing up the local curry house and ordering a lamb bhuna.

'Your name, sir?'

'My name?'

'Yes, sir, for when you are collecting.'

'Just tell them Cobra is coming... and he's angry.'

Things men learn from *Top Gun*:

• To succeed in any sort of male environment, you must win the support of your peers not the bosses. Witness the moment Maverick is told off for performing a brilliant but dangerous manoeuvre in training. Although chewed out by his bosses, it doesn't matter because one of his fellow pilots leans in at the debriefing and whispers to him, 'Gutsiest move I ever saw, man.' Who cares if you lose your job? As long as you're the cool guy in the room, what does it matter?

• Aviator sunglasses will NEVER go out of fashion. In fact, they're only going to get more popular. By the 24th century all males will have them automatically grafted onto their faces the moment they complete puberty.

• There is no such thing as a 'hard deck'. I don't even know what a hard deck is but I know that Maverick and Goose don't care about it. 'Hard deck my ass' they whoop at each other. I think the moral of this is, if a rule exists, then it's there to be broken. Just don't go too far, my friends, I think the police might be willing to overlook a few minor traffic infringements but I don't think they'll take too kindly to you shouting 'Speed limit my ass' in their face and high-fiving your mate in the passenger seat.

• *Top Gun* is useful in explaining how men make friends. If you meet a man and you hate him instantly in the way that Maverick hated Iceman the moment he saw him at the pilots' bar in the first bit of the film, you're probably going to end up being his best mate. Think about it. Why do you hate him? Because you're jealous of him and you want to be like him. Iceman was jealous of Maverick's natural talent and Maverick was jealous of Iceman's ability to keep his emotions under control. By the end of the film Iceman utters the immortal line to Maverick, 'You can be my wingman,' and they end up best buds. I'd like to think that they served out the rest of their military service flying dangerous missions together and when it was time to retire they joined Ryanair and spent their days knocking off Polish air hostesses.

• In life, sometimes you have to limit your expectations. Not every business deal is going to be successful, not every girl is going to give you her number, sometimes it's going to be too close for missiles. That's when you switch to guns. I don't know what that last bit means, but the next time someone catches you mucking something up, and you don't have a readily available excuse, just say, 'Hey, it was too close for missiles, so I switched to guns.' They'll be too baffled to challenge you.

8. LETHAL WEAPON

One of the best ever buddy movies, starring Danny Glover and Mel Gibson as a pair of mismatched cops. Gibson plays ex-Vietnam vet Martin Riggs, who lives in a trailer on the beach. He is a suicidal cop teamed up with family man Roger Murtaugh, who lives in a palatial house with a boat in the front drive. It's the classic tale of opposites thrust together. Men love films like this because it's a tried and tested formula. Although *48 Hours* with Nick Nolte and Eddie Murphy is considered to be the first-ever buddy movie, *Lethal Weapon* was the first smash-hit buddy movie. What is it about *Lethal Weapon* that makes it so special? Probably the fact that it's about two characters who at first don't like each other. Riggs is always trying to make Murtaugh do stuff he doesn't want to do. The immortal phrase often copied in other inferior films – 'I'm too old for this shit' – was forged in the fires of the *Lethal Weapon* quadrology. Except it's actually pronounced 'I'm too old for this shhhhiiiiiiiiyyyyytttt'.

Films like this are so good, men are often willing to overlook the glaring inaccuracies in them. According to the dates in *Lethal Weapon*, Riggs the supposed Vietnam vet would have actually been 13 years old if he had fought in the war. I know he's supposed to be a hard bastard but please...

Lethal Weapon is just the same as most men's relationship with each other at work, except for the fact that we work in nondescript offices and factories while they work on the mean streets of LA. We all know a guy at work who's been there for years and only wants to get on with his job, but we're always sending him stupid emails or getting him to come to the pub at lunchtime. Granted we never get him involved in solving crimes which lead to a bomb being planted under his toilet but you get the idea. Men like to antagonise other men. Riggs and Murtaugh are the best example of this on the big screen.

Things men learn from *Lethal Weapon*:

● If you ever want anyone to think you're crazy, just dart your eyes around manically for a bit. For the first half of *Lethal Weapon* I genuinely thought Mel Gibson had a squint.

● This film taught me that if I ever have to take on a heavily armed multinational drug-running syndicate, I shouldn't worry too much as all the henchmen tend to have glaucoma. Even a one-armed blind man with Parkinson's couldn't miss Mel Gibson in that film. He had a mullet so large it has its own postcode.

This film is probably what *The Odd Couple* would have been like if they had had guns.

7. SWINGERS

One of the best damn comedy movies ever made with barely a bum scene or a wasted line. Vince Vaughn is fantastic as the hyper cool and confident Trent and Jon Favreau really nails the insecure and recently dumped Mike. Although it is a film about relationships, it manages to captivate and entertain by pretending it's not. It's about a guy called Mike who has recently been dumped by the love of his life, and his best friend Trent who tries to lift him out of his misery.

Swingers is useful for us men because we can watch this film as a guide to dealing with women. A significant scene in the movie deals with how long a gap should you leave before you call a girl after getting her number. Numbers are bandied about. One day is too keen. Two is 'too anxious'. By the end of the scene it's agreed that three is the optimum number of days. Now, I would never have known that in a million years, so it's useful for guys like me who don't have a clue. (Although if you're taking tips on dating from a film you're pretty much in dire straits anyway.)

There's a scene in the film where Mike gets the number of a girl he really likes and ignoring everyone's advice about leaving a cooling-off period before ringing, he dials her number as soon as he gets home. He then leaves a horribly awkward message. He rings back straight away to try and tell the girl to ignore the last message. He puts the phone down and then rings straight back to try and explain that he's not weird even though he's just left two messages despite only just meeting her. This continues for a good five minutes, each phone call more cringeworthy than the last, until the girl finally puts him out of his misery and picks up the phone and tells him never to call her again. EVER. This scene should be shown at school to teenage boys, with subtitles flashing across the bottom of the screen that say, 'This is what happens if you use the telephone to talk to girls!' Telephones reduce us to blithering idiots. They should only be used to arrange where to meet a girl. That's it.

Swingers is a great buddy film because it is so like real life. All our friends give us advice about what we should do with women but the best thing to do is to completely ignore them.

Things men learn from *Swingers*:

- It gave us the phrase 'pulling a Fredo' (as in *The Godfather* when Fredo enjoys relations with two cocktail waitresses).

- Men sit around and mope when dumped. Badly.

- Three days. Standard time before calling a woman.

- Women always come back to you just as you're getting over them.

6. BUTCH CASSIDY AND THE SUNDANCE KID

One of the greatest buddy films of all times, it stars two superstars in their prime, Robert Redford, before his face started to develop crevices the size of small countries, and Paul Newman, before he became strangely obsessed with salad dressing. They play two likeable outlaws in a changing age, hunted down by a ruthless posse who signify the end of an era. Many men identify with this film because they just want to be left alone. Now I'm not suggesting wives and partners are like a determined posse relentlessly hunting down their prey but certain comparisons can be made, and to be honest that scene in the film where they jump off the cliff into a raging river is probably what I'd be prepared to do to avoid a Saturday afternoon shopping trip.

The two of them are ridiculously good-looking in the film and they dominate the screen like no other duo since. The film opens up with Paul Newman (Butch Cassidy) being challenged for the leadership of his 'Hole in the wall' gang by a minion. He agrees to have a knife fight with him, but simply turns round and delivers one of the best kicks to the nuts I have ever seen in a film. There is nothing that can grab a man's attention more in a film than a big fat kick in the testicles. Get 'em hooked with that at the beginning and you've got a captive audience for the rest of the film.

Once they manage to get away from the homicidal posse, they decide to up sticks and make a go of it in Bolivia. It's the big fish in a little pond idea.

Things men learn from *Butch Cassidy and the Sundance Kid*:

- The director has kindly put all the romantic bits in soft sepia focus so it's a clear signal that nothing exciting is going to happen any time soon, which enables us to get another beer from the fridge or go for a pee.

- Sundance obviously didn't take swimming lessons at school and have to pick a rubber brick up from the bottom of a pool in his PJs.

- Robbing a Bolivian bank and trying to pull it off speaking Spainish is not a good idea.

- Bolivians apparently all pronounce Mr as 'Meeeeest-air'.

- Sundance is one of the few men in history to almost pull off wearing a tash. Almost.

5. INDIANA JONES AND THE LAST CRUSADE

The father and son. It's a double act that rarely works in films, apart from *The Passion of the Christ* (undeniable chemistry there). Dr Jones is back again for the third instalment of the saga. This time he's brought his dad... er, also Dr Jones. It was a masterstroke casting Sean Connery as Harrison Ford's dad even though he was actually only twelve years older than Ford. We all know that once you've flown the coop it's hard to find common ground with your dad. You need things like fishing trips, family dinners or football matches to enhance bonding sessions. What better way to get reacquainted with your dad than by fighting the Nazis together.

Things men learn from *Indiana Jones*:

- Archaeologists don't earn much and need a second job.

- Never trust a monkey. Especially a Nazi one.

- Real men have a bullwhip on them at all times.

- TV show *Time Team* gives archaeologists a bad name. Indiana Jones would have punched Tony Robinson in the face, with his whip.

4. DIE HARD: WITH A VENGEANCE

America's unluckiest cop John McClane is back, this time dealing with a preening baddy called Simon (Jeremy Irons having the time of his life, you feel), who loves riddles and whose brother John threw him off the highrise in the first *Die Hard* movie. Oh dear.

McClane is forced into a friendship with Samuel L. Jackson, who plays Zeus. Zeus is better at solving the riddles Simon sets them. I still don't understand the four gallons of water one. Please someone help me.

Naturally there is the scene with the mandatory giant bomb and a really handy giant digital timer counting down. Wires have to be cut. I don't know about you but most men do love a good bomb defusal scene. From our man McClane to Jack Bauer and James Bond. The great red wire-blue wire conundrum is a staple of man movies. There has to be a TV show in it or an Oscar category.

Things men learn from *Die Hard: With a Vengeance*:

- Bombs are filled with highly explosive pancake syrup.

- You can use a mobile phone under a federal reserve but not going through a tunnel.

- Simon + helicopter + M60 machine gun vs. McClane + revolver + 2 bullets is NO CONTEST.

- Saving your wife twice from terrorists won't guarantee that she won't dump you.

3. SONS OF THE DESERT

This film was made in 1933 and is still a masterpiece of comedy. I'm a huge fan and have been since I was a kid. Laurel and Hardy are the kings of comedy. Ricky Gervais told me he has nicked so much from them, and he claims that he and Stephen Merchant are even built along similar lines. Ricky's little plaintive looks to camera owe their origins with Ollie. Just genius, the pair of them. Talk about buddy movies. They try to get some buddy time away from their domineering wives (Stan's is one of the best duck hunters around and a crack shot with a gun) and go to the 'Sons of the Desert' convention in Chicago. Illnesses are faked so they can have a boys trip to Honululu. Chaos naturally ensues. They are terrified of their wives and there is nothing sadder to see than men getting caught out in a lie. Mates are supposed to give buddies an out, to sometimes fall on the grenade for them. This doesn't happen.

Things men learn from *Sons of the Desert*:

- In the 1930s, kicking a woman in the butt was OK.

- Don't marry a woman who is a crack shot with a rifle.

- If you have lied to your wife about where you've been, try not to come home singing a song about where you really went.

- Any man could mistake wax fruit for the real thing.

2. TANGO & CASH

'Two of LA's top rival cops are going to have to work together... Even if it kills them.'

What a movie from the eighties. Sly Stallone is Raymond 'Ray' Tango. Kurt Russell is Gabriel 'Gabe' Cash. With a double header like that the movie's got to be good, right? Tango and Cash is something else. If an alien came to earth and wanted to see one film to show all that was good and bad about the eighties, I would probably sit him down, get him some Angel Delight and make him watch this. Two cops who hate each other, framed for a crime they didn't commit (familiar theme in the eighties – see *The A Team*), thrown in jail together and the rest you can work out yourself, I'm sure. A young Teri Hatcher plays Tango's younger sister and obviously Cash tries to hit on her.

Things men learn from *Tango and Cash*:

- The best way to break your fall when sliding on electric power cables 90 feet in the air is to just land on your knees and you should be OK.

- This maximum security stockade lets you keep your belt should you need to slide your way out on electricity pylons.

- Gabriel Cash leaves his door unlocked for the convenience of assassins.

- English accents are apparently the same as Australian ones.

- Great eighties buddy cop movies should always have an excellent opening first half, followed by a pile of faeces-style ending involving an unbelievable police vehicle and a whiny-voiced hobbit.

1. MIDNIGHT RUN

I know I said this list is in no particular order, but I lied. This is number one. This is the holy grail of men's movies. It's the classic 'buddy' movie.

Starring Robert De Niro and Charles Grodin, Bobby boy is a bounty hunter who has to bring Grodin in. They are polar opposites as in many buddy movies but over time they form a friendship. The final scene always leaves me misty-eyed, not for what is said but what isn't. Grodin takes off his hidden money belt with over $300,000 in it and hands it to De Niro, who has been hounding him for the entire movie but is now letting him go. By letting him go, De Niro won't be able to claim the much-needed bounty for turning Grodin in. Faced with the offer of the money belt, De Niro just says: 'I don't know what to say...'

'You don't need to say anything.'

The pauses and looks say it all. This is how men are. No hysterics. It always has me in tears. Big man tears. As does a scene earlier when funds are running low as De Niro is forced to try and get some cash to help him bring Grodin back. He has to visit his ex-wife and see his daughter, whom he hasn't seen for years. His daughter runs after her dad as he's pulling away and tries to give him her pocket money. Despite being broke and out of luck, he refuses. I'm welling up already just thinking about it. It just melts your heart and says more about dads and daughters than any chick flicks (that said, I love *Parenthood*).

I read an interview with Echo and the Bunnymen lead singer Ian McCulloch, who said this was his favourite film because, 'It's about everything. Man's soul, his honour, and his dignity. I watch it and think that's how I want to be.'

This movie is one every man should own. When I was interviewing Matt Damon about the latest *Bourne* film last year, I happened to mention *Midnight Run* and he came alive all of a sudden. Apparently he and his buddy Ben Affleck are obsessed with this movie. He even has the poster on his wall. I hope, though, that doesn't mean it's due for a remake by them.

Things men learn from *Midnight Run*:

- You can suffer from something called fistaphobia.

- Doughnuts are for good news and bad news.

- You can spot shifty work colleagues as they will have dodgy facial hair.

- Trust De Niro. If he says he's gonna bring someone to LA by midnight Friday, then he's going to do it. Don't send a rival bounty hunter after him.

TELEVISION

That's Hollywood sorted. But since the late fifties, it hasn't always been necessary to go to the cinema to get a fix of testosterone. Television also provides a vital role in the glorification of man. Here are just a selection of the amazing men on our screens from the last 50 years.

BODIE AND DOYLE FROM THE PROFESSIONALS

To this day I still remember the first time I saw an episode of
The Professionals. I was eight years old and it was coming to the
end of its life. My mum was out and Dad had fallen asleep on
the sofa so I used this lapse in bedtime security to gain access to
the forbidden watershed TV programming. Martin Shaw's perm
had lost its sheen and Lewis Collins's wry smirk was beginning
to look tired, but they still had it. I was too young to understand
the intricate plot details, but even at that tender age I grasped
the basics. Two really hard men in a fast car went round
chasing criminals and international terrorists. My eyes goggled
at the violence. But the sheer manliness of the characters
delighted me.

People laugh at me when I say this but I think Kiefer Sutherland
has ripped off Martin Shaw in his portrayal of Jack Bauer. We've
all seen episodes where Jack interrogates terrorists with that
amazing technique of speaking ever so softly, 'Where is the
bomb?', and then repeating the same phrase at 50 decibels louder.
'WHERE IS THE BOMB?' Well, he got that off Martin Shaw. He
spent all five series of *The Professionals* playing Doyle like a
schizophrenic. One minute he's as nice as pie. The next Bodie's
having to hold him back because he wants to shoot dead a
shoplifter. Bodie was a different creature, though, hard as nails
and cool as ice. His greatest weapon against villains was of course
his pout. Just one look at his devastating good looks and they
would surrender to the authorities. I have a friend who is a 100
per cent heterosexual but maintains that given the chance he
would have sex with Lewis Collins.

There was no real explanation as to what CI5 was, but the makers clearly wanted it to be a cross between CID and MI5. So you could get the exciting spy stuff without all the boring Cold War politics, the thrilling hunt for the bank robber without the boring detective work, the electrifying interrogation procedure without the suspect 'falling down the stairs'. And of course there was another element to *The Professionals*. The boss. Gordon Jackson playing George Cowley, a bluff, brusque Scotsman who let them get on with the job without interfering too much. I always thought he was more like a crazy PE teacher than a boss of a major governmental agency, but there you go, that's TV for you.

What really got me hot, though, was the fact that Bodie had once been in the SAS. It was often mentioned and just that whiff of danger and the fact that he might have actually killed a man and worn his ears as a trophy added to the general excitement of the whole series. To this day, sometimes when I go shopping, I lean out of my car window pretending to be Bodie, surveying the mean streets of Surrey like it was the London Docklands. (That's where most of *The Professionals* seemed to be shot.)

MAGNUM PI

The moustache, the Ferrari, the Dobermans, *Magnum PI*. What a show. On the face of it, Thomas Sullivan Magnum IV had the sort of life you dream about. He had a job looking after a multi-millionaire's mansion in Hawaii but actually didn't have to do anything, got to come and go as he pleased and had sole use of the mansion's Ferrari. Watching it gave me an unrealistic sense of how easy life was going to be for me in later years. I had a very rude awakening in the first ever careers seminar I went to: 'What do you mean there's no jobs in Hawaii hanging out in bars, shagging lots of women and driving a Ferrari about? Can't I at least go and work in Rick's bar and work my way up? No? I'll even clean the Doberman's shit off the front lawn if it gets me in the door.' That wasn't all. You remember how Tom Selleck would always state with some conviction that 'I never get involved with my female clients' and then be necking with them in the next scene? Yeah, well, I thought that would be a foolproof technique with the ladies. One minute I'd be professing absolutely no interest in them, then I'd lunge at them manically. It may have worked for Magnum but all it got me was a good few kicks in the plums. It also gave me the impression that every American over the age of 30 had been either a) in Vietnam or b) in a covert government organisation or c) in both. I also marvelled at the fridge and the fact it was always stocked with beer at any time of the day. Never mind tracking down underworld bosses, Magnum's first case should have been finding out who mysteriously restocked his fridge when he wasn't looking. It also astonished me that he could be on the trail of the bad guy in denim hotpants, Hawaiian shirt and a big red Ferrari and still remain inconspicuous to the villain.

JOEY AND CHANDLER FROM FRIENDS

The saga of Joey and Chandler was possibly TV's best portrayal of a relationship between two best mates. It was tender without being schmaltzy, and they had great reclining chairs. It's part of a man's life to at one point share a flat with an absolute nutjob, and that's the nucleus of Joey and Chandler's relationship. How many of us can relate to Chandler getting upset at Joey's construction of a giant 'entertainment unit' that partially covered both bedroom doors? Everyone has that mate who spends too much time messing with his graphic equalisers and subwoofers. I have a mate who almost convinced me about replacing the cables connecting my stereo to the speakers with better ones made of kryptonite or something. Talk to the hand! If you have a mate who is into his stereo, here's a fun thing to do. The exact moment they leave you alone with the sonic beast, mess with all the levels and graphic equalisers. I do this every time I visit his house. It's got to the point where he keeps a sheet of paper with all the settings on it.

It was the fact they lived without limits that captivated me. They got rid of the dining table and replaced it with table football, kept ducks in the flat and watched *Baywatch* on reclining chairs. We all wish we could live like this but in reality it could never happen. You'd drop curry sauce or bits of pasta onto the table football men until they could turn no longer, the ducks would be drowned in the bath when you get upset at them for dumping on the carpet again. Joey and Chandler's life can only ever be a dream to mortal men like us. But what a dream.

FRED AND BARNEY FROM THE FLINTSTONES

The Flintstones was a smart TV show ahead of its time. A cartoon show aimed at grown-ups, a proto-Simpsons if you like. Fred and Barney were next-door neighbours and best mates, which is rare these days, and one reason I like the show so much. I harbour fantasies about becoming mates with my next-door neighbour. Instead of curtly nodding at each other when we occasionally take the bins out at the same time, I'd like us to pop into each other's sheds and talk about our favourite tools. I'd like us to be able to hide out in the local pub when our wives have some sort of neighbourhood get-together.

Both were members of some kind of Masonic organisation, the Loyal Order of the Water Buffalo Lodge. Fred helped his mate Barney learn how to play golf; they bought a burger joint together. When Fred dumped Barney in the annual Water Buffalos sports competition for Joe Rockhead, Barney gave Fred a black eye (on which Fred put a huge raw bronto steak). Like with any TV buddies, they were very different characters. Fred was the jovial one with a gambling problem (just the mention of the word 'bet' would have him stammering) and Barney more thoughtful. But the really big question is: Wilma or Betty? Two very fit cartoon women, but which one would you rather? This was actually discussed in *Red Dwarf*. Lister and The Cat agreed that Wilma Flintstone was 'the most desirable women who ever lived'. Cat went on to say he would go with Betty but would be 'thinking of Wilma'. The whole thing is then disregarded as stupid. Lister says 'She'll never leave Fred and we know it.'

MINDER

A classic TV show. I loved this as a kid. You wanted to be just like Terry. A man's man, a former pro-boxer who had done time but had a heart of gold. This show is an all-too-often overlooked classic. My CDT teacher would have us watch it as homework and then there would be a test the next morning about last night's episode. Now that's education! Stick shows like this and

The Godfather on the national curriculum to ensure the young people have a grounding in the classics – forget *Middlemarch*, you need *Minder*.

(Dennis Waterman had also, of course, starred in the classic *Sweeney*. *The Sweeney* was and still is THE HARDEST TV SHOW EVER, a TV show name-checked in songs by Kate Bush ('Wow') and The Squeeze ('Cool For Cats').)

Terry, in the early years of the show, would often pull what was then referred to as a 'dolly bird' so most episodes had some generous half nudity. As time went on, he got laid less. Arthur was pretty mean to him, though clearly loved him. *Only Fools and Horses* creator John Sullivan has said that he used *Minder*'s success to get the BBC to commission his show.

Minder also gave us the phrase ''er indoors' and had one hell of a theme tune, sung by Dennis Waterman himself, which he performed on *Tops of the Pops*. I think more stars should be encouraged to sing their own theme tunes. *24* is great but a theme tune done by Kiefer would be awesome. He wouldn't have to do the whole thing – maybe just a rap à la John Barnes in 'World In Motion'.

Catch me if you can cos I'm the Bauer man

We must defend and attack, hit them and hurt them

We're playing for CTU, CTU, CTU

Same with *Lost*. That has no theme tune at all. A Sawyer and Jack duet with a rousing guitar solo from Kenny Loggins could be a number one hit around the world.

CAPTAIN KIRK AND OFFICER SPOCK FROM STAR TREK

These two were a legendary act. The spod and the stud. Many of us have a mate who is way better-looking or cooler than us. Or someone who is a bit of a nerd and smarter than us. You don't ever want a mate who is both.

Captain Kirk got the big boss's chair up front with the giant plasma screen; Spock was more aloof being that he was a human/Vulcan mix. I'm not a Trekkie so I'm not sure of the exact percentage split of human to Vulcan Spock was. (I'm guessing he was like the 'polyester blend' you see on that tag thingy you get in clothes.) He could also do a 'mind meld' and a school playground favourite, the 'Vulcan Death Grip'. Tuck shops across the land would have big lads doing the 'Vulcan Death Grip' on skinny lads like me.

Spock's mum was human and his old man a Vulcan called Sarek. His mum was called Amanda. It must have been hard growing up with your dad a Vulcan alien. Being purely logical in all his dad behaviour would have meant poor young boy Spock would never have seen his old man behaving oddly around bonfires or suddenly going berserk and accusing you of playing with the radiators in the house. I don't think Spock even had a surname and so if he played football I guess he would have been referred to as 'Spocko' or 'Spocksey'. He had a seven-year mating cycle which would explain his death-like grip.

Captain James T. Kirk was a legendary swordsman and the *Enterprise*'s inflight stud, seducing Orion slave girls and gender switching shape shifters. Many fell for the Captain. He may even have spread some STDs around the galaxies they visited. He never seemed to carry any protection with him and with those tight uniforms we'd have known. He also had an enormous cock. No, I'm not a pervert but he was packing some serious phaser heat down there. The tightness of his pants showed no visible panty line. Was he going through the twenty-third century commando? With advances in freeze-frame technology you can, should the need ever take you, even see if Kirk was a Roundhead or a Cavalier. But this is not the concern of a highbrow book like this – any more of Captain Kirk's penis could harm my chances of being in Richard and Judy's Book Club.

I'm not sure if it was Spock or Kirk's decision that all the women on board wore very short skirts. I guess the HR department didn't really exist then. All the doors on the *Enterprise* were very noisy too. You would have thought a smart man like Spock would have got a little WD40 on them.

Surely he could have found a better uniform for the boys to visit other galaxies in than spandex. That stuff can really chafe. And if you got a little unwanted pant tent action going on, there was no hiding place. They had no pockets either. Where do you put your keys or how do you fiddle with your balls?

I also felt that they never really looked after that great ship either. How many times did the polarity get reversed? That's got to wreck the engine. 'Giordi, reverse the polarity and we'll have trap one back in business in no time.' The *Enterprise* mechanics must have gone nuts. 'Which one of you little fuckers has been reversing the polarity willy nilly? Gonna have to change the spark plugs again now.'

Remember when there were no seat belts in cars and you would just get flung around in the back? Smashing you into the doors and your little brother or sister. Or rearranging your face in the back of your dad's seat whenever he touched the brakes. Good times. Same with the *Enterprise*: for a while they had no seat belts and Kirk and the lads would have real fun slamming on the anchors while travelling at warp speed, with no fear of being flashed by an intergalactic speed camera. Then some kind of seat belts were fitted that seemed to just buckle up the legs and no other part of the body. That's if you were on the bridge and were lucky enough to even get a chair. Sure, Captain Kirk's entourage got them but many were just standing around. Waiting to get the dreaded call-up to go visit a new planet, knowing full well they would die if they were wearing a red shirt.

Star Trek was also not too realistic with the use of the holodeck. Put men with a machine that can effectively recreate three-dimensional scenes and I can tell you now it wouldn't always be Wild West saloons. I don't need to go any further but that deck would need to be wiped cleaned regularly. By a red shirt.

Kirk was replaced by very different captain. A new-age man. With no hair. Not as macho and someone who could act. Jean-Luc Picard, as Kirk before him, was a product of the times. Men were supposed to be more sensitive and caring like Jean-Luc. Kirk seemed outdated. But here's the question: who was the ultimate captain, Kirk or Picard? Or put better, you're part of an expedition team on the *Enterprise*, you're a red shirt so will probably die, but which captain would you want going with you to give you the best chance of survival?

First, let's be honest here. Kirk was a reckless son of a bitch with his crew and often endangered their lives. Picard is more cautious, level-headed. He liked Shakespeare. Kirk liked whisky. Picard had the great catchphrase, 'Make it so, number one.' But 'Beam me up, Scotty' trumps that, surely? Picard could outwit the Borg and then enjoy a nice cup of tea. That said, Kirk would have shagged three green alien babes in the time it took the kettle to boil. Picard went for quality in a mate rather than the horny cowboy Kirk going for quantity. Kirk wasn't fussy and would happily do the nasty with someone green. Kirk was never scared of throwing down with an alien being and going toe to toe in a fist fight. Picard seemed a little gun shy. Picard is a Frenchman despite the English accent. This has to be taken into account. After debating this with my wife, who is a massive *Star Trek* fan (I hesitate to say Trekkie as I don't believe she is a virgin), and my Trekkie in residence Kimron, here are my other reasons why Kirk is the ONLY CAPTAIN:

- Two words: Shoulder Roll. Nobody does it better than the K man.

- Kirk doesn't wear dresses when admirals arrive for lunch.

- Kirk once said: 'I've got a belly-ache – and it's a beauty.'

- Kirk would never sing to children in a crisis.

- Kirk, almost single-handedly, repopulated the Earth's whale population.

- Kirk never pretends to be a barber in order to gain a tactical advantage.

- Kirk looked better in a ripped shirt, sweating.

- If Kirk ever met a Ferengi, he would rip off its head and shit down its neck.

- Kirk never once said, 'Abandon ship! All hands abandon ship!'

- Kirk has a cool phaser – not some girly Braun mix-master.

- Kirk once fought a Greek god. And won.

- Picard's bridge appears to be beige. Kirk's wasn't.

- Picard allows cats on board, while Kirk beams away even really cute things, like Tribbles.

- Kirk specifically ordered a swivel Lazy-boy for the bridge.

- Kirk travelled through the Great Barrier, met God, and wasn't even impressed.

- Kirk would never let his Chief of Security wear a pony tail.

DEL AND RODNEY FROM ONLY FOOLS AND HORSES

I know they are brothers but no serious list of men and men in TV shows could be complete without Del and Rodney. *Only Fools and Horses* might seem a bit naff and dated these days but some of the scenes and lines are comedy's finest. The blow-up dolls, the chandelier, Boycie, Trigger... I could go on. The relationship between Del and Rodney is bullying, nasty, mean and touching, like most of our relationships with our best mates.

FLETCH FROM PORRIDGE

One of my favourite sitcoms ever. Bear in mind it was made in the 1970s and you have to appreciate how edgy it was to have a BBC sitcom about men behind bars. The first episode is one of the greatest opening episodes to any TV show (*Lost* had another great first episode) with Godber spending his first night in prison and Fletcher looking out for him. Ronnie Barker was a comedy genius and the one-liners are classics. The storylines were too. Richard Beckinsale could not have been any better as Fletcher's wide-eyed innocent cell mate. Fletcher really cared for Godber, despite his brash exterior. Like a typical man he would never say so but we all knew he loved him like a son. Fletch was the wise mate we all want to turn to in trying times, always trying to get one over on the guards and fellow screws. Like when he replaced the governor's ultra-soft toilet paper with the sandpaper-like stuff the prisoners had to make do with.

The rest of the cast featured some of this country's finest talent. Fulton Mackay as Mackay was terrific, as was Peter Vaughan as the truly menacing Grouty. Grouty scared the hell out of me as a kid; you got the feeling he could do something awful at any moment. The normally unflappable Fletch was scared of him too.

At the beginning of this book I suggested that it might be our parents' fault that we are the way we are. Now we see it's not just them. It's also Captain Kirk. And over-exposure to *Top Gun*.

VIII

THE FUTURE OF MEN

In about 125,000 years, two things will happen. The Rolling Stones will be on their final tour and men will cease to exist. That's right, we are dying out.

The man chromosome, the Y chromosome, is failing, and according to eminent Oxford geneticist Brian Sykes will eventually disappear. In 125,000 years' time. It gets worse. Our man juice will not be good any more either. Sperm counts are falling. Experts aren't exactly sure why but it has to be something to do with all these sequinned TV shows every Saturday night. On ice, in ballrooms. Men behaving sadly.

In a few years' time, women will be able to have kids without the aid of a man and our most basic function – procreation – will be redundant.

The child will always be female.

My fellow men, it could all be over. The game's up.

At the house party of life we are drinking the last warm beer and all that's left to chug is an out-of-date bottle of Amaretto. And one of us has just told the neighbours to fuck off.

IMAGINE A WORLD WITHOUT MEN

They reckon prison populations would drop by 95 per cent and there would be a 70 per cent drop in road deaths. No wars.

In a post-manageddon world there will be no more barely cooked chicken at barbecues. No wasted time driving around lost. No piles of clothes on floors and watching TV fearing that at any moment someone with attention deficit disorder will start flicking around. There wouldn't be any funny smells on long car journeys.

How boring does the world without men sound?

I think to survive we need to make some changes and man up. I also think maybe we need a major redesign. Maybe women could team up with Apple and give us a redesign to make us more socially acceptable. This would give us a few more years. We need the iMan.

Our biggest design flaw is the penis. It leads us astray. A detachable penis is clearly the best way forward. You could hand it to your wife for safekeeping on a boys night out. She could keep it under the sink. Men would be frisked for hidden penises and have to walk through penis detectors at nightclubs or bars. There could even be a nationwide penis amnesty. Like with guns in America, your penis would be kept in a locked cabinet at all times and have a registered owner. Though this could lead to men having to try and sneak their penis out of the house:

'Where are you going with that?'

'This? Oh, just off to see the lads.'

'Then you won't be needing that. Put it down.'

Remodelled into the iMan, we could also be downloaded. This way, when we are asked what we are thinking about, women would finally be able to find out. And then never bother to ask again as the truth is discovered... Nothing. A handy reboot button on us would help when we crash or zone out and need firing up again to come online. I see problems, though, with women spending too much time calling overseas helpdesks because their iMan just sits around scratching his iBalls.

'Have you tried feeding him something?'

'Tried that. Nothing.'

'What's happened in the last few hours?'

'Nothing much, really. Oh, he watched England play and they lost I think.'

'I'm sending someone out right now. He's flatlining... We don't have long.'

No, we need something bigger and more far-reaching. Luckily, men, I have a plan.

To save ourselves and mankind we need to set standards and may I now introduce my man-saving idea...

THE MAN CARD

All men should have to apply for a statutory man card and then carry it on them at all times. Our standards have fallen and to survive we need to behave in a more manly way. To earn this important documentation, a man should fulfil a few basic requirements. This would ensure that men start to behave more like real men and not metrosexuals and Radio One DJs.

To earn your man card you should:

- Know your car engine size

- Know the size of your TV

- Watch *The Godfather* (I and II, never the unspeakable third) at least twice a year and always be ready to be randomly tested on your Godfather knowledge by any man-card-carrying man

- Be able to cycle with no hands

- Never EVER wear low-slung denim

The man card can be taken away for violations. Men would be able to report other men for behaviour not becoming of any self-respecting member of the male community. Going to see *Sex and the City* would result in immediate execution. There would be a 24-hour anonymous man card violation line.

'Yeah, hi, I've just seen my neighbour Bob allowing his wife to turn the burgers on his barbecue…'

'Er, hello? There's a guy in my office who wears way too much cologne.'

'Just seen someone on the train blatantly wearing a man bag.'

On the other hand, perhaps we should just embrace our decline with with a firm handshake and pat on the back (not too firm a handshake – men who do that usually have very small dicks). It's 125,000 years away so what's the point in worrying about it now? It could even be used to your advantage. Tell your other half that you are dying out. She might feel sorry for you and have sex with you.

Here's to the next 125,000 years.

IX

THE REAL MEN FIRST XI

I'm always wishing I was a hero, but these days no one else seems to think that's anything to aspire to. I blame TV. Most teenagers' idea of doing something heroic is to get on *Big Brother* and perform a sex act live in front of millions. In my youth all the best TV shows had a charitable nature to them. *The A Team*, armed only with machine guns made from BA's jewellery and some cabbages, helped impoverished farmers get their land back. The Green Cross Code man taught a whole generation how to avoid death under the wheels of ice-cream vans (although personally I wouldn't feel comfortable leaving my children under the supervision of a six-foot West Countryman in a green leotard hanging around schools).

These are the people who taught me the true meaning of manliness when I was growing up. Yes, that's right: George Peppard, Mr T and Dave Prowse shaped my life. There doesn't seem to be anybody like that in the public eye any more. Heroes now have to be cynical and sneering to be popular. Or they're troubled by being special like the cast of *Heroes*. We need to get back to basics and teach people what it means to be real men again. There should be a school set up with a staff of bona fide heroes to tutor the next generation in man studies.

I want to see Gene Hackman circa *The Poseidon Adventure* in a classroom demonstrating to students how to shout 'Get them to safety' while sacrificing himself in a room of boiling steam. I want Arnold Schwarzenegger installed as the head teacher. Self-sacrifice is the most important part of heroism, so each day at assembly he would address the school while lowering himself into a pool of molten metal just like he does at the end of *Terminator 2*. And of course the hero of Glasgow airport John Smeaton would be the school PE teacher. Except he wouldn't waste his time on sport. He'd just show us how to kick terrorists in the nuts. This subject of great men and the lack of them in modern society came up over a few cold beers with some mates. I then had a brainwave, or beerwave. It was a way of taking our arguing over who are the truly great men to the next level.

Pick a football team of inspirational heroic manly men. Plus manager. Who's in your team?

There are rules.

- No actual footie players

- Can be dead or alive

- Real and fictional players allowed

You can waste so much time arguing about your team selection. I did. I'm getting nervous about showing you mine but here goes.

First up, the most important person in the team and the man who has the hardest job, the manager. (It's also hard because he's the one who usually gets interviewed by Garth Crooks.)

MANAGER: WINSTON CHURCHILL

Every team needs a manager and who better than the tactical genius who masterminded the classic victory over the Germans in 1939–45, Sir Winston Churchill. This form gets him the big job.

This team of men needs a manager not afraid to forge ahead when everyone else says he's wrong, and a manager who can inspire his team to battle on when all seems lost. And someone who can drink a bottle of port every day. Defeating the most evil empire the world has ever seen is a hard enough task, but while you're a bit woozy? Now that deserves respect. Winston Churchill will provide the backbone for the team. Imagine his half-time speech...

"We will fight them on the halfway line, we shall fight them for the the corner flag, we shall fight them to get the lucky dressing room, we shall fight them in the queue to get a pie at half-time, we shall never surrender... unless they get an away goal... then we're screwed."

This team needs somebody not afraid to give out a tongue-lashing once in a while. Good old Winny was the greatest exponent of the put-down in the last century. Once at a ball, feminist Nancy Astor remarked to him that, 'If you were my husband I'd put arsenic in your tea.' Quick as a flash, he replied, 'And if you were my wife I'd drink it.'

This wasn't a fluke. Another time, while heavily incapacitated due to an excessive intake of brandy, he bumped into a female MP, Bessie Braddock.

'Mr Churchill, you are very drunk,' she said.

'And you, Bessie, are ugly. So very ugly. But in the morning I will be sober, whereas you will still be ugly.'

A man with those verbal skills is very valuable in any dressing room. But most of all he had that winner's mentality which is essential in any manager. Plus he had a budgie that lived on his dinner table.

GOALKEEPER: HENRY VIII

If Winston was our greatest leader then Henry VIII was the greatest king. Well, for men anyway. You may have the image of a portly ginger megalomaniac but as a young man he was a virile and fit sportsman. He would hunt regularly and he was an early tennis enthusiast. Sometimes both in one day. I'm not sure if he used his racket to hunt with but it does give me an idea for Extreme Tennis.

A man of his size would be the perfect person to go in goal. Almost like Neville 'the bin man' Southall but with his own army and navy. Henry VIII is the Gazza of this team. Every team needs a tragic Stan Bowles-type figure and Henry VIII is that man. He inherited a rich kingdom and had all the talents to take him to the top but instead he pissed it all away by shagging everything that walked and regularly ate his own weight in meat. By the time he died aged 55 he was so fat the coffin he was in burst its sides and he had to be packed back in like jelly into a mould. What a way to go. Hail King Henry. Watch out for those crosses, Your Highness.

LEFT BACK: COLUMBO

Have you ever met anybody who's said they don't like Columbo? No. Because everyone does. He'd probably be rubbish at clearing headers, what with only one good eye and all, but his determination would be amazing. Columbo's like a Jack Russell. He never lets go.

The opposition striker would break through the defence and be about to slot the ball past Henry VIII, who probably wouldn't actually be standing in the goal but rather at the pie stand. But anyway, there he'd be, about to whack the ball in, foot poised for the coup de grâce, and suddenly he'd get a tap on the shoulder and he'd turn around to hear that immortal phrase:

'Just one more thing...'

Before he knew it, instead of scoring the winning goal he'd be admitting to murdering his art dealer because he'd refused to help him defraud his rich aunt out of millions. Columbo's in the team because he represents that never say die attitude you need in a successful football side. He's the underdog. Also, one of the best things about Columbo was you never saw his wife. He would mention her all the time but never actually brought her out. No worries about Mrs Columbo turning into another pain in the backside WAG. The world's greatest detective gets the call-up.

CENTRE BACK: MR T

Simply put, Mr T is one of the greatest men alive today. A walking, talking bad ass, he's in my team as a towering centre back. Every team needs an enforcer and Mr T is that.

But he wasn't just muscle. He was an engineering genius. Imagine for one minute our football team of great men is up against a side with low morals. Portsmouth. This team is getting a thrashing and at half-time decides to lock our team of heroes in the dressing room. Oh no! How will we get back on the pitch without forfeiting the match? Step forward, Mr T. He would gather together all the old orange segments and use the changing-room baths to ferment them into pure alcohol, which he would then use as fuel for an improvised armoured car he had made out of old lockers, with rolled-up gym mats as wheels. He'd then bust through the changing-room walls with a cannon made from shin pads which fires corner flags.

They say never meet your heroes as you'll only be disappointed but meeting Mr T was one of my favourite interviews. One question I asked him was:

'If the A Team van was about to fall off a cliff, and you could only save one member of the gang who would it be?'

I expected he'd say Murdoch but instead I got the greatest answer to any question I've asked in my entire career. Rather than try and put his answer in my words, I've gone back and listened to the tape and transcribed it word for word for you and future historians.

MR T: 'I'm a tell ya, brother, that's a good question.'

ME: 'Thanks.'

MR T: 'But because I'm so dedicated I'd save 'em all. It would be a miraculous thing, you know. Something that nobody would ever have seen before. Y'know tha A Team knew how to whip up gadgets and make things. So while they be drowning I'd take off all my gold chains and connect them one at a time and then I'd hook 'em together to make a big gold rope and throw it to them, cos if I put 'em all together to make a rope it be about 50 yards. AND I'D THROW THIS GOLD LIFE PRESERVER TO 'EM AND SAY "HANNIBAL, GRAB A HOLD, MURDOCH, GRAB A HOLD, FACE MAN, WRAP IT AROUND YOU. AND IF I LET ONE OF 'EM DIE, I'D HAVE TO COMMIT SUICIDE MYSELF COS WE A TEAM. AND LET ME TELL YOU THERE'S NO I IN TEAM, BUT THERE'S SURE AS HELL A T IN TEAM!"

I honestly think they should disband the United Nations and let Mr T sort out global conflicts. Forget international diplomacy, all you need is both countries in a room with the man himself and he'd bang their heads together (literally) until they settled their differences. That's why he's in my team. Although he'd miss out on some away matches due to his fear of flying (like Dennis Bergkamp) but that's a small price to pay to have the baddest man on the planet in your team.

CENTRAL DEFENDER: THE GODFATHER (CAPTAIN)

In every team there's a go-to guy. The one man that speaks to the referee, the man who decides which player takes the penalties, the guy who lines up the defensive wall. In my team it's the Godfather. Don Vito Corleone. Imagine the scene: one of my players, let's say Columbo, has cut down a member of the opposition (a badly mistimed tackle due to the glass eye) and is about to be sent off by the referee. Don Vito sidles up and makes him 'an offer he can't refuse' and, hey presto, not only is there no card, he's awarded a free kick to us.

I did consider putting a different Mafioso in the team, Tony Soprano, but he might be too brutal. I want honour and manliness restored to the beautiful game but I don't want to see Tony Soprano trying to beat a centre forward to death with his shoe, just because he didn't show his cousin 'some respect' in the players' lounge. That's a step too far. Still, it would have been nice to have had the girls from Bada Bing as cheerleaders. No, Don Vito is the man for me. Just keep him away from the half-time oranges.

RIGHT BACK: DICK DASTARDLY

First of all, before we get down to it, there were a couple of cartoon characters that came close. Like Top Cat. I really liked the idea of having a team with Top Cat in it. But the more I thought about, the more I realised it wouldn't work. For a start, Top Cat is not a team player. When the opposition attacked, could I really count on him to shore things up at right back? Or would he be cooking up a scheme with Benny in the changing rooms? Also he's a cat. A top one but still a cat. He'd probably spend most of the match licking his balls and crapping in the 18-yard box. Sorry, Top Cat, you didn't make the cut.

In the end I opted for a cartoon character I've loved ever since I was a child. Dick Dastardly. I think the *Wacky Races* needs a Quentin Tarantino-style makeover. A big movie version of the *Wacky Races*. Ricky Gervais, with that dirty great laugh of his, would be perfect as Mutley.

What I liked the most about Dick was his desire to win at any cost. That's the sort of spirit I need in this team. Sometimes digging a trench 20 feet deep and filling it with piranhas, barbed wire and broken glass is what needs to be done.

Let's be honest, when we're 1-0 down in the 90th minute and Henry VIII's thinking about whether it's pheasant or partridge pie for dinner, Dick Dastardly will be surging forward looking for that equaliser. Scratch that. He'll be in a bi-plane spraying poison over their defence to give our guys a clear run on goal. GO DICK.

LEFT WING: JAMES BOND

James Bond is going to be in defence as I need someone unflappable and resolute, and a man with enough nous to diffuse a nuclear bomb, while simultaneously chatting up a diplomat's wife and getting measured for a Savile Row suit.

Has to be Sean Connery. Daniel Craig is a brilliant Bond but can only drive an automatic so Sean gets the edge. He's such a man's man and commands so much respect he's the only actor ever allowed to keep his normal accent no matter what nationality he's playing. In *The Hunt for the Red October* he played a Russian submarine commander with a Scottish accent. In *The Wind and the Lion* he played a Moroccan chieftain with a Scottish accent. And in *Highlander* he played a Spaniard with a... you guessed it, a Scottish accent. That film was even stranger because Frenchman Christopher Lambert played a Scot with a French accent. In *The Untouchables* he was supposed to play an Irishman but sounded like a cross between Frank Carson and Billy Connolly.

Anyway, the real reason why James Bond is in the team is because he's the greatest male character ever created. He lives the life us ordinary men can only dream of. One minute defeating international arms dealers at poker, the next boffing glamorous women on a Caribbean beach. And for that added bonus on the football pitch he's exceptional at breaking through impenetrable fortresses. Honourable mentions also go to the other action man types who wanted to get into the team. It was all about the 'JBs' really. Jason Bourne. Good effort, lad, but come back in five years when you're ready. Jack Bauer. Look, mate, you're good, everyone knows that. But what is it with you and the fact you can't follow simple orders? I don't want to see Winston Churchill telling you to man-mark a midfielder, only to have you blow up the stadium and then kidnap the referee because someone's trying to frame you. You came within an inch of actually being selected for the team, only to mess it up by insisting that all the boot boys were Al Qaeda spies and torturing them. For this team, I'm sticking with the original and best JB. Jimmy Bond.

MIDFIELD ANCHOR: THE HOFF

The Hoff takes his rightful place in this team slap bang in the midfield. I'm going to play him in a holding role, as the man is huge. I met him years ago when he came into my radio show and the guy is literally seven foot tall. I admire David Hasselhoff for many reasons. One of them is his impressive television career, which we'll come to later, but a good reason for him to be in this team is the fact he single-handedly brought down the Soviet Union with nothing more than his singing voice and a puffy black silk shirt. Although Russia was in decline around about 1989, the Hoff sure as hell wasn't. When he journeyed to the border between East and West Germany to stand on the Berlin Wall and belt out his hit songs (well... hit song, anyway), by the end of the night it had fallen. That's the sort of man I want in my team. He said to hell with politics, to hell with bilateral talks and to hell with the Red Army, I'm going to sing a cheesy electropop song entitled 'Looking For Freedom' to the East and West Germans and they'll both be so moved they'll tear down the wall and unite the country instantly.

I scoff at some of his detractors who say the wall was knocked down by people from West Germany trying to escape his singing. Pop star, actor AND forger of nations. That's not the only reason he's in the team, though. He is one of the world's most awesome actors. *Knightrider* had everything a television show needed. A crime fighter who dressed all in black, kind of like Johnny Cash but taller, and er... a talking car. Not many actors can make a relationship work with a camp talking car called KITT. The car was Michael's wingman and buddy. What man wouldn't want a talking car that could drive you home from the pub?

His other seminal TV show, *Baywatch*, also played an integral part of my youth for reasons that don't need to be explained to any man between the ages of 20 and 50. In fact, it would be great to have the Hoff in my team just because the *Baywatch* girls could be standby first-aiders. Imagine Pamela Anderson or Erika Eleniak bouncing all over the pitch with the sponge and bucket for a lucky injured player. In slow motion. The spectators would love it. Each match would be a sell-out for that alone. I just hope the Hoff doesn't invite that weird male lifeguard from the show. You know, the one with the moustache who was always lurking in the background of every scene. There was something wrong with him.

David Hasselhoff aka Michael Knight aka Mitch Buchannon aka liberator of Germany, please take your place in the First XI of Greatest Men.

MIDFIELD: MUHAMMAD ALI

The greatest sportsman of the twentieth century strides into my team easily and he's never even played football. Muhammed Ali was blessed with being both witty and an amazing fighter. He had that rare ability of turning boasts into achievements by his sheer will and determination. I don't want to get all heavy here but Ali is more than just a sportsman. He really is an inspirational man. He became heavyweight champ of the world and gave his belt up after refusing to go to Vietnam. Why? 'No Viet Cong ever called me nigger.' Do yourself a favour and watch *When We Were Kings*. His humility, humour, talent and charisma have never been equalled in any sport since.

In my little home office where I'm writing this, I have a huge framed Ali print. He looks great, shadow-boxing in his white trunks. There is one of his classic quotes on it:

Champions aren't made in gyms.

Champions are made from something they have deep inside them – a desire, a dream, a vision.

They have to have last-minute stamina, they have to be a little faster, they have to have the skill and the will.

But the will must be stronger than the skill.

Beats the usual 'the boys done good', doesn't it?

RIGHT WING: RAY MEARS

Not many of us know how to do manly things any more. Except for one man. And this one man is single-handedly holding the thin red line against repeated and ferocious attacks from the metrosexuals. Their battle cries of 'I don't know how to gut a fish!' and 'Do you have any mung beans, shopkeeper?' are no use against his knowledge of wild berries and his big knives.

Ray Mears. The survivalist who can make a three-storey house out of soil is one of the greatest living Englishmen. He can hunt. He can track. He can fish. He can find his way across a desert using only a shoelace. If you described Ray Mears on paper you'd think he was a craggy-faced, muscular Red Indian dressed in moccasins. What makes him brilliant is he looks like most British men. Chubby and middle-aged.

Before I'd let him on the pitch I'd make sure he built the team dugout from leaves and bits of berries. Once that's done, I'd set him to work on the right wing. Not attacking the ball or trying to score. Building a bear trap to capture opposition players.

But why should his survivalist skills ensure him a place in the team? Well, remember that kid you used to play football with who nobody really liked, but he played anyway because he had a ball? Ray's that guy. If the ball gets punctured he could patch it up with goose shit or something. Or even better, he could make us a new one from a badger's scrotum, stitched together with squirrel tails.

Ray, get your bitch tits over here. You're in.

STRIKER: STEVEN SEAGAL

Three words: Hard. To. Kill. One of the greatest films ever made. Steven Seagal is shot several times at point-blank range with a shotgun and goes into a seven-year coma. A nurse tends to him during this time, attracted by the size of his penis, which apparently doesn't alter during a coma. He wakes up and tracks down the baddies who killed his wife. He also finds the son he thought was dead. Their reunion is the stuff of cinema gold. He ruffles his hair and then snaps the neck of a guy. What a dad! There isn't a film of his I don't own. Some of the greatest comedies ever made. Even Michael Caine co-starred in one of his seminal classics, *On Deadly Ground*. Caine started the film with an American accent then wisely dropped it ten minutes in. Seagal beats up a pensioner in this film but that's nothing compared to the scene where he makes a hard-arse redneck cry in a bar fight, then delivers the immortal line: 'What does it take to change the essence of man?'

This man is a legend. The life of Steven Seagal should be made into a book and that book should become the new Bible, Koran and Torah all rolled into one. He's achieved every single thing a man should accomplish in his life from starring in million-dollar movies to having his own energy drink (Steven Seagal's Lightning Bolt. I'm not sure of the ingredients but it's probably made by wringing the sweat out from his pony tail). Steven Seagal is not a man of words. He's a man of action. Which is why I'm making him one of my strikers. Every aspect of his life is action-packed. Just look at his film titles and you'll soon realise most of them only have three words to them.

- *Hard to Kill*

- *Out for Justice*

- *Above the Law*

- *On Deadly Ground*

- *The Glimmer Man*

- *The Belly of the Beast*

- *Half Past Dead*

'Aha!' I hear you cry. 'What about his best film, *Under Siege*? That only has two words.' You're right. It was a rare mistake from the sacred man. But he went and corrected that mistake with *Under Siege 2*.

And for those of you that say his film titles are short so they can fit his increasingly chubby face on the poster, I say shame on you.

It's the naked aggression of Steven Seagal that's ideal for my team. Most teams have a nutcase that likes to poleaxe men for no good reason, and Seagal is mine. Seagal does have a softer side, however. He's been a practising Buddhist for over 20 years now. In that space of time he has actually tried to turn himself into the Buddha, as you can see by his expanding waist size and the fact that his face is so bloated it looks like someone has attached a bicycle pump to his head and been squeezing air in since 1988. It's this Buddhism which has led him to claim a sense of understanding with nature and that a dog warned him about a fire at his house once. He also said the Mafia tried to threaten him into letting them be in his movies. You can't blame them. Did they lean on De Niro or Brad Pitt? No. they wanted screen time with the best. Seagal.

These days his movies are actually too good for general release and go straight to DVD, like the recent great *Pistol Whipped*. One critic said it should have been called *Pizza Whipped* due to Steve's 'big boned-ness' but that's cruel.

STRIKER: FRANK SINATRA

The first and only musical entry into the team, Frank Sinatra. Effortlessly cool and suave, the man cut a swathe through the musical world for over 60 years. Every team needs that naturally gifted player who makes it look like he's making no effort whatsoever, a Le Tiss, and I think Frank Sinatra fits the bill.

I can imagine him in the six-yard box with a cigarette dangling out of his mouth, Martini in hand, dressed in a tuxedo, ready to stick his foot out if the ball happens to come his way, allowing him to poach the undeserved equaliser.

Also, Frank could help the team out off the pitch with the football song. For every 'World In Motion' there's a 'Diamond Lights'. For every 'Three Lions' there's an 'Anfield Rap'. Imagine Frank ushering the squad to a recording studio, getting Seagal out of the canteen and teaching Mr T the scales. He'd bring in a big band and my football team would record a stone-cold classic that would be sung in the stands of Wembley Stadium for years to come.

Frank comes from a bygone age where you couldn't be cool by buying expensive clothes or splashing your cash around. You couldn't get everyone to adore you by going on a reality TV show. You had to have natural cool. And when he scores the winning goal, after the players carry him off the pitch on their shoulders (not as a celebration – he had trouble walking towards the end), he'd whisk all of us over to Vegas. What a guy.

That's my team. Who's in yours? Don't even try and poach Seagal.

Manager: Winston Churchill

Henry VIII

Dastardly   Mr T   Corleone   Columbo

Mears   The Hoff   Ali   Bond

Seagal   Sinatra

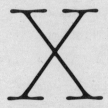

THE MEN COMMANDMENTS

We may be messy and disorganised but men need and like rules. Not instructions, rules. Instructions are to be ignored, that's a man rule. We all know that one, right? No man in their right mind has any business looking at the instructions; as in flat-packs, so in life.

Woman: Didn't you read the instructions?

Man: No.

Woman: Well, where are they?

Man: I dunno...

Rules help men navigate this uncertain and changing world. It's easy to understand why we love some rules, like the offside rule, because they mark out our territory and stop women spies from infiltrating our favourite sport. Others, like why a man should never tell another man his flies are undone, aren't so easy to explain. (You didn't see anything, if asked.) But rules there are and they show how a man should behave in certain situations. These rules are not actually written down anywhere or ever spoken about.

Much as I enjoyed Daniel Craig as the new Bond in *Casino Royale*, a man rule was blatantly broken. Any woman watching it wouldn't have noticed it, but I did. **Real men don't wear Speedos**. Ever. We all know the scene I'm talking about. Bond steps out of the sea like we all did many years ago at the dawn of Manvolution, in a pair of Speedos. He's also setting a bad example for the rest of us. The ladies see Bond looking like that, then they see the whey-faced dough boy they are with and they feel let down. Real men never wear Speedos. It rhymes with paedo for a reason. Someone should have stopped him and reminded him of the man rule concerning acceptable swimwear. He really should have known better.

The rules are there to protect us, and without them we're all in trouble. They aim to govern a man's behaviour both when he's with his mates and alone.

No man can explain why he must change the television channel every three seconds if he is in possession of a remote control, but he must. In the same way that penguins have it in their DNA to travel miles and miles every year to exactly the same spot in the Antarctic to lay eggs, man DNA dictates we never look at another man's penis at a urinal. These rules can't be explained but they exist and we cling to them.

The Men Commandments are here for the first time in print. Please read them, commit them to memory, then tear out the pages and eat them.

MEN COMMANDMENT I

Find Your 'Cave'
[Thou shalt have no other
God than the remote control]

Life was easier when we had caves. Cavemen hung out in them, chatting, hunting, drawing on the walls and crapping in the corner. There was no flat-pack furniture, there were no walls to paint 'eggshell' and no loo rolls to replace. Good times.

I'm no historian but I guess annoying sales calls were limited to cave-to-cave sellers offering kitchen flints and clubs with more rounded grips. Easy monthly repayment plans started as low as five bearskins a month, although I bet the salesman would mumble, 'Your cave is at risk if you can't keep up your repayments.'

All of man's crucial evolution took place in caves, which is why we need one even to this day. But modern society contrives to take that away from us. How many of you have your own personal space in your house/flat/squat/cell/secure unit? All too often you get given a corner of a room, or a couple of shelves somewhere in the basement or loft. Maybe your partner has allocated you some space above the U-bend in the bog. For man to be truly happy, he needs Man Space.

You may need to mark out your territory in your house. The living room is often the best place to start. You can mark out your boundaries like dogs if you want but in this day and age that's unnecessary and may affect the warranty on your nice DFS sofa. Unless Linda Barker is now offering pee-resistant covers for men.

THE UNINTERRUPTED VIEW

Start with the most important item of the 'Cave': The Chair. You must place your chair in a position to give you the best view of the television. There should be nothing blocking your view. If there is, boot it out of the way, even if it's living and breathing: wives, pets and small children included. I practise a form of feng shui in my living room. I call it **man shui**.

Basically it means I shove everything in my way to the other side of the room. Our cave ancestors didn't make the camp fire and then seat themselves looking away from it. (I'm also right in thinking they didn't have small camp fires either. They had roaring widescreen heat definition ones.) Once the chair is in position, there's one important rule to remember: NO MAN SITS IN THE CHAIR BUT YOU.

If sticking your penis in another man's wife is unacceptable, sitting in his chair is perhaps a worse crime.

The only exception is if you *formally invite* another man to sit in it, just to try it out. He must accept your invitation, in writing. A third party needs to witness this too.

The chair has to be very comfortable, obviously, but please stop short of fluffy cushions or throws. The chair should be a place from which you pontificate and hold forth, delivering sermons about things you know little about to anyone but often only to the TV screen. What's important is that you have a throne. Remember how your dad used to lean down from it and clip you round the ear? It's like that. This is the piece of furniture that partners hate

the most – which makes it even better.

I'm sure even Angelina Jolie gets the hump with Brad's chair.
I doubt whether poor Becks is even allowed one. Maybe now he
just has a diamanté booster seat.

Unfortunately some of us can only dream of one day having
that special chair. Right now I'm having to do with a bit of the
couch. I'm between chairs and one of the reasons for writing
this book (other than trying to save mankind) is to fund a proper
man chair. It's the place we go to unwind and relax. Even dogs
are given a bed. Digby my dog has one and I'm sure I have
caught the little fella smugly looking at me saying, 'You don't
even have one of these, therefore I'm the daddy in this house.'
I then have to remind him that I still have my balls. He counters
this with, 'But you walk behind me carrying my shit in a
sandwich bag.' We both laugh at this stalemate and agree to
leave it there.

Most of history's great rulers did great things while sitting on
their thrones. Jimmy Savile fixed it for hundreds of kids from a
chair which handily also dispensed cigars. Joey and Chandler in
Friends had the greatest form of chair, the recliner. Davros, leader
of the Daleks, wrought havoc from his chair. He actually went one
step further and made the chair part of his lower body.

Take away a man's chair and chaos reigns. Look at the state of the
news these days. Is the rubbish coverage because of falling
production budgets and the public's political apathy? NO. It's
because the newsreaders don't read the news sitting down any

more. They stand. They perch on the desks. Sir Trevor McDonald looks like he's lost in some sort of computer game.

It's another attempt to feminise us.

THE ENVIRONMENT

Once the chair situation is sorted, turn your attention to the immediate area around it. Are there any scented candles within ten feet of your space? If the answer is yes, then remove them immediately. They should only be used by men for two things:

1) If you want some sex

2) If you've farted and want to disguise the evidence.

American Indians used to leave the bones of their prey around the boundaries of their territory to dissuade unwanted visitors. We now do the same with unwashed plates and items of dirty clothing. If you're challenged about this and the fact that you live like a pig generally, explain it's what the Red Indians did.

THE ONE GOD

With the addition of a television and a stereo system (the larger the better on both counts) the modern cave is pretty much set, apart from one other thing. Some would say the most important thing in the whole cave: **the remote control**.

It's a man's third arm, his extra limb. Look at the evidence. If you suffer an industrial accident you get the highest payout for thumb damage. The insurance companies say it's because you wouldn't be able to do manual labour without a thumb. Bollocks. It's because you could never use a remote control properly again.

The remote has superseded the spear as the most likely thing to be found in a man's hands at any one time. Well, that and his penis. It's all we have left. The highest state of Manvana is for a man to be sat in front of the box with one hand on the remote and the other down his pants rummaging (see Commandment 2).

When we lose the remote, the desperation to find that thing is palpable. I spend more time turning the place upside down like the FBI in some killer's lair than if I just changed the channels by hand.

REMOTE ENVY

Now women have two types of penis envy to deal with: the normal one and the one that makes it hard for them to watch *America's Next Top Model* without us flicking around the moment the ads come on. (The simple reason for the constant flicking by the way, girls, is *we need to see EVERYTHING that is on*.)

Thou shalt covet thy remote and channel-surf annoyingly. Forget Lorena Bobbitt, the best way to castrate a man is to take away his remote control. It really is the worst crime imaginable, which is why women enjoy doing it. Meanwhile, the supposed government do nothing. Any woman who wilfully steals her man's remote should get FIVE YEARS IN PRISON. NO REMAND.

There are so many things we could be watching at any one time and for women to deny us this opportunity should be illegal. It's certainly immoral. I have two young daughters whose world I have flooded with every noisy, flashy toy imaginable. What do they make a beeline for? My remote. I'm sure my wife is secretly training them behind my back.

We've all been there when a woman flounces in and snatches the remote from our hands like a demented banshee and turns it over to *Corrie* or *Desperate Housewives*. Their excuse is that we're not watching anything. Technically we're not. But how do you explain that you were planning on spending the next half-hour doing the following:

- Watching 30 seconds of motocross on Eurosport. Even though you have little or no interest in it.

- Flicking through all the music channels, pausing for no more than 1.4 seconds on each one.

- Starting to watch a film on a movie channel, the moment you realise Gene Hackman and/or Michael Caine are in it.

- Starting to watch a programme on a channel, realising it's nearly over and getting disappointed, but then getting elated when you realise you can watch it on the +1 option. Then realising it's not going to start for another 20 minutes then getting bored and turning over.

- Watching five minutes of the Audi channel.

- Watching ten minutes of the History Channel documentary about the Nazi's funniest home videos.

- Flicking through all the music channels again but this time cursing out load as they all have adverts on at the same time, except for VH1 who have 'Footloose' by Kenny Loggins on a 24-hour loop. Thankfully.

- 'Accidentally' stumbling upon the free Television X preview.

- Watching five minutes of CBeebies, where what appear to be giant aliens made entirely of flannel babble away at each other. Starting to drool and nod off. Scratching balls. Wiping dirty crisp hands on couch.

- And then moan nothing is on.

How can you explain all this to a woman who wants to simply sit through a boring soap? You can't. This is why possession of the remote control is vital. Never, ever give it up.

MEN COMMANDMENT II

Bodily Functions and Touching Oneself [Thou shalt nudge according to thy want and need]

It's a man's fundamental right to touch and/or adjust his man bits. Let's call it 'nudging'. This behaviour starts at a very early age before less important stuff like learning to walk and talk.

Scratching our bits is pure joy for men. Every man has seen a cat or dog take this a step further and actually lick his own balls. If we could, we would. The late great comedian Bill Hicks thought that this might be our next evolutionary step. If he's right, the work rate from men is going to suffer drastically. Sick rates will rise and men could find themselves being asked to leave department stores if they start doing it in public.

Although technically we should be free to nudge whenever and wherever we want, as with any other man behaviour, it's open to abuse. I'm sure we can all think of someone who is a **serial nudger**.

Might be that weird family uncle around the young nieces doing handstands or it might be the 'you want black pepper?' man in a restaurant who nudges throughout taking your order. It's not right. It's a known fact that men from the continent nudge more than British men. I think it's the climate or something.

NUDGING AND THE LAW

In fact, one of Italy's regional courts has recently attempted to *ban* nudging in public places. This is an outrage. We may need to come together and campaign for our Italian brothers. A Nudgers Pride march on Number 10.

The Italian ruling came about after a 32-year-old workman from Como was convicted of indecent behaviour and the judge said it had been proved he had been seen '*ostentatiously touching his genitals*'.

This is taking away a fundamental man right. A mandamental right. The right to touch and nudge our balls. In private is best, in public it should only really be for minor adjustment as is sometimes needed. Surely there must be something about nudging in the Geneva Convention? We may need a Maneva Convention to protect these basic man rights.

Even more so if you are aware that, according to Italian folklore, a quick grab of the organs protects against bad luck. Now I know

NUDGING: YOUR THREE-STEP PLAN

It is our God-given right to give our balls a scratch and a readjustment any time we want to, but it must be done properly to stop other people getting the wrong idea. Here is how it should be done to avoid confusion:

Step 1: Move your hand forcefully to the crotch area. Don't dilly dally, don't look furtive, otherwise people with mistake you for a sex offender. Hesitation is the enemy of the 'nudge'. The earlier you commit yourself, the earlier you'll be finished.

Step 2: Make the necessary movement. It could be a simple scratch. It might be that you want to move 'the package' from the one side of the trouser leg to the other, you might even want do some tucking, but whatever you do, get it done quickly. Work to the rule that 'anything more than five seconds and you're playing with yourself'.

Step 3: Finished? Then get the hell out of there. Get your hand above waist height ASAP. Now this is the most important bit. Look around and check to see if anyone has seen you. If they have, chuck them a grin. This will tell them that you have noticed their concern and this grin will reassure them. If it's in public, NO POLISHING. That's strictly for behind closed and possibly locked doors.

why footballers grab each other's in the wall before a free kick. Apparently any mention of national disasters or diseases will also bring about a flurry of cock-rubbing action from Italian men. Must be interesting watching the TV news: any bad news story and the anchorman has to put hand under the news desk for a cheeky nudge. Not sure what Sir Trevor McDonald or Nicholas Witchell would make of all this. Even funeral processions passing by get the crotch grab salute. Which all goes to prove that touching your penis doesn't have to be sexual. Men do it for a variety of reasons.

The workman's lawyers said that it was 'compulsive, involuntarily movement probably to adjust his overalls'. It seems a likely reason. How many times have you worn a pair of jeans slightly too small for you and found that you are pawing at yourself like a dog with mange?

In another man's 'cave' it's perfectly normal to nudge. However, you must wait for the owner of the cave to nudge first. It's the same rule with breaking wind. *Little Britain* star David Walliams was once on my radio show and, seconds before we went live on air, broke wind violently. The correct etiquette would have been to wait for me to 'break the seal' first with a 'tommy squeaker', which then gives him a signal to join in if he wants. He blamed it on a glass squeaking as he moved it on the desk but I don't buy it. He's now barred.

THE BOGS

Toilet etiquette is a minefield for men. Only this year a man in New Zealand was given a prison sentence for punching a man.

URINAL RULES - OK?

1) You never make any small talk to another man in the toilets. A barely perceptible nod may be given.

2) Eyes front at all times, no peeking at another man's penis or even the man himself.

3) It's your responsibility to ensure there is a buffer of one empty urinal between you and the other guy.

4) When urinating against a stainless steel trough, direct the flow away from any other participants and remember the splash-back factor on stainless steel is 40 times higher than on standard porcelain urinals.

5) It is permissible to try and shoot down the pubic hairs on the rims of the urinal, provided there are no other men in the immediate area. (However, it is unacceptable to try and play football with the orange disinfectant balls. That's just childish.)

6) It is OK to avoid washing your hands, but only if you are trying to make a quick exit because a drunk man is trying to make conversation with you.

7) If said drunk is trying to talk to you while you're still at the urinal, you must stare at the advert in front of you like it's the word of God itself and no amount of small talk could ever possibly force you to take your eyes off it.

His crime? What his lawyer said was 'a breach of urinal etiquette'. He tried to talk to the man in the toilet.

So let's take it step by step and start with the Men Commandments concerning men's urinals. We know that when you enter a toilet and you are faced with a wall of possible urinals, you must take the one furthest away from any other man. This is just the start of it. The rest of the rules which may NEVER be broken are shown opposite.

I have to admit that I broke one of these rules once. And it was the cardinal one about checking out another man's tackle. I was in the toilets at a music awards ceremony and suddenly Bono was using the urinal next to me. Now I know I said earlier that you must never look at another man's package, but there is an exception to every rule and for this one it's if you're famous. So I had a cheeky little look, and worse than that, he caught me gawping at it.

He turned to me and said, 'You trying to see if it says Sony Corporation on it?'

Which you have to admit is very funny. I almost forgave him the *Zooropa* album. Almost.

All these rules cease if it's the toilets at a man event. Especially a football match. I know someone who became a hero for this one line spoken out loud at the urinal trough at an Arsenal match. Some of the funniest banter happens at football matches. Some of the most moronic too. This man was at the steel trough when it all went a bit quiet among the usual excitable chatter about the referee suffering from possible myopia when in walks a policeman. Like a deflated balloon, the atmosphere changed suddenly when our friend in the big pointy hat and high-visibility jacket emblazoned with 'POLICE' for the hard of seeing and intelligence (we *are* talking Gooners here) strolled in. He took his position next to my friend and all eyes were front, trying like you do in these situations, to see out of your eyes. My friend casually looked at him and said clearly and loudly for all those present to hear:

'Do you know where I can buy any drugs?'

Hilarity did ensue. Even the policeman pissed himself. In a manner of speaking.

Men spend a lot of time in toilets, at home and at work, so it's only fair that we should be familiar with the rules that govern them. I hope this section has been useful to you all, and remember, the next time someone tries to talk to you at a urinal... eyes front!

MEN COMMANDMENT III

Men and Cars
[Thou shalt not be the prick in the back]

After women and mates, the most significant thing a man has a relationship with is his car. In fact, some men have better relationships with their cars than with their wife or girlfriend.

I mean, look at Michael Knight in *Knightrider*. He had a better relationship with KITT than any of the ladies in the series. He never let him down, or had a go at him for getting shitfaced and eating burgers drunk and shirtless. He was the perfect car. Michael could get hammered and sleep it off in the back, while KITT drove him home.

Apparently both men and women remember more about their first cars than their first kiss. I can believe this. I remember the stunner that I first got serious with. She was burgundy with come-to-bed headlamps, although like most women she had trouble starting in the morning. Peugeot 205, 999cc and she was gorgeous. I often think about what happened to her. Where she is now and whether or not she thinks about me. She was a right dirty bitch as well. She used to spray oil all over the road. Sadly all good things come to an end. When I got married my wife insisted I got rid of her. She part-exchanged it for the car that cannot be named as I'm too embarrassed to admit ownership but it's Swedish and safe and about as much fun as driving around in a tractor.

WOULD YOU LIKE A CHAMOIS WITH THAT, SIR?

Cars are part of a man's heritage. In the old days you could look out of your window on Sunday morning and see all the dads washing the family car. My dad was no different. He'd be out there every week with a bucket of warm soapy water, wearing his Dad Pants. If you're not familiar with Dad Pants, they were trousers that your dad stepped into on a Friday evening and removed only after *Highway* on a Sunday night. They were usually made of brown corduroy or a polyester blend resistant to water, fire, acid and small explosions. They gave them special magical dad powers. In fact the US military are developing a war plane right now manufactured from Dad Pants material.

I've recently started to wash my car on a Sunday. Well, I did it once. I went to Halfords and did the typical man thing of going over the top. These places are like an Aladdin's Cave for car men. Sad car men. You see men in Halfords who seem to have been there for months, just wandering round touching things and trying to justify spending money on a *Special De Luxe Le Mans Genuine Chamois Leather* – 'Only £39.99'. (Why do they need to put 'genuine' in there? Is there a black market in counterfeit chamois leather? If so the government needs to act and declare a war on the illegal trade of chamois leather. Come on, Bono and Sting, we need a World Chamois Day. Let's get some chamois wrist bands to help raise awareness.)

I went in wanting to buy some cloths and a bucket. I left £80 poorer owning a *Le Mans Special Car Cleaning Kit*, with five different cleaning fluids. One even for the mud flaps, I think. What a jerk. I went home and instantly become obsessed with using *all* of the five different cleaning agents and almost had a complete mental breakdown as the cloths were not working well and there were visible smear marks and I was starting to lose my mind. My wife locked the front door and told the kids to come away from the windows so as not to see me like this. I didn't even have a pair of Dad Pants on. To this day it's only been used once, which is the cause of much amusement to my wife.

So what have we learnt? There's no need to spend your child's university fund on supplies to clean your car. My father used a bucket, an old shirt cut up into rags and a couple of squirts of washing-up liquid and vinegar (another substance our parents believed was some sort of miracle juice – it could do anything from cleaning surfaces to curing syphilis). Times have moved on and we have car washes and plenty of people who are happy to do the job for you for a fiver. (Why is it that when they offer to clean your car it seems more like a veiled threat than a sales proposition?) Let them and save your soul.

WHO'S THE PRICK IN THE BACK?

If you think about any great male-orientated TV show, the rule is the sexier and more heroic the character, the better the car. Magnum PI had a Ferrari, DCI Gene Hunt has his Audi Quattro, Morse has his Jag and Michael Knight had KITT. It's vital to the role. When Bodie and Doyle were rolling across a big sexy car bonnet in hot pursuit of a suspect or nonce, it wouldn't have looked half as good if it was on an Austin Allegro.

A big question for man etiquette is asked when men have to share a car. First big question: who's driving? 'Who cares?' you may say but it's an important question to ask. For those who think this isn't a big deal, take a look at this news story:

> A police officer punched a colleague in the face following a
> 'petty squabble' over who was going to drive a force van,
> Newport Crown Court has heard. PC Byron Emerson-Thomas,
> 37, wanted first go in the van at the start of a night shift because
> it was fitted with a new radio, the trial heard.

Brilliant. You can imagine the scene.

'My turn tonight, remember.'

'Don't think so. You were supposed to drive it yesterday.'

'Yeah but yesterday was a Bank Holiday, we weren't here. You said I could have first dibs on the new radio.'

'Tough shit.'

'Gis the keys.'

'NO.'

'YES.'

'NO.'

'YES.'

'NO.'

Punch.

It may seem like a petty reason for a fight, but the point is that the driver is also the alpha male. It's not just an argument about who's driving the car. It's about who the boss is. I've always wondered how the police decide who drives; now we know it's just a big old fist fight. Do ambulance and fire engine drivers have the same problem? I wonder. Perhaps that's why ambulances always turn up an hour late. They've been scrapping over who gets to turn the siren on.

It was always the cool characters who got to drive the car. I used to be allowed to stay up late and watch the odd episode of *Starsky and Hutch*. Hutch always drove the mighty Ford Torino, and on the rare times he let Starsky, he seemed very unhappy. I don't think Morse even let Lewis near the wheel. Fred always drove the Dream Machine in *Scooby-Doo*. Then he and Daphne shagged in the back while the others solved that week's shenanigans. That last bit might not be true but that's what my hormonal young brain imagined. Han Solo flew the *Millennium Falcon*; Chewie didn't even get a look-in as he'd probably get hair all over the dashboard. The only exception to the rule was Captain Kirk on the *Enterprise*. Technically he didn't do any of the driving but he did the next best thing and told Chekov where to go. Kirk did occupy the driver's seat and he never once told Chekov or Spock to take the wheel while he went for a slash.

THOU SHALT ALWAYS TRY TO BE THE ONE DRIVING

Three men approach a car. They're friends, have been for many years. They've been through highs and lows together. However, as they approach the car, two of them start trying to move towards the car faster than the other. Why? What's going on?

They're fighting to get to the front passenger door. The driver is the owner of the car. What's up for grabs is the title of co-pilot. Wingman. Shotgun. What's left for the loser is a fate worse than death. The *MUMBLY SEAT*.

No one wants to be the guy in the back. You have the driver, then the co-pilot, who is in charge of audio entertainment and navigating duties, then the mumbly in the back who has *no* responsibilities.

Nothing.

Just left to stare out of the window forlornly at other men in cars also in the idiot chair in the back. Sometimes desperately popping up in the no-man's-land canyon between the two front seats.

'What's that you're laughing at, guys?'

'Oh nothing... Can you sit back, I can't see out the rear-view mirror.'

If you find yourself in this position then you truly are no better than a ginger stepchild, relegated to the naughty step. Then there's the other really bad thing about being in the back. All stereo systems are set up to have it loudest in the rear, so you'll be forced to either man it out but with ears bleeding, or degrade yourself by asking the pilots up front to *turn it down a bit, please*. Never put yourself in this position as it will almost certainly demote you in the pecking order of your social circle. Children and dogs sit in the back. Not men.

The A Team neatly got round all man class division by having captain's chairs in the back in a bid to lessen the blow of not riding up front with Mr T and Hannibal. In cop shows any informant is chucked in the back. It's for losers and grasses. Which one are you?

There is a great story that Bill Wyman used to be the only Rolling Stone up front in the van (this is in the early days of the band, unless I have totally misunderstood this story and the Rolling Stones still travel the world in a Transit van) on the grounds he got travel sick in the back. Smart man. Mick, Keef and Ronnie in the back cramped. Bill happy up front. Then he got rumbled as they realised he was in the back once and hadn't shown any visible signs of his travel sickness. He showed his hand. What caused Bill to forget his little ploy? He was in the back with a girl.

THE WINGMAN; GOOSE

If you are the co-pilot then you abide by the rules concerning this important role. You are in charge of navigating. That means:

- Never having the map anywhere within easy reach or even giving it a cursory glance.

- More important are the sounds. If you make mix tapes as I still do (yes, I know that makes me a sad man but mix tapes still rule) there's an art to it. I know it can be done now on a CD or iPod but that's too easy. If Apple brought out a huge clunky piece of kit the size of a door for old-school tape-to-tape recording and mix-tape making it would be a bestseller.

You do not start the singing in the car. The driver does that. Never leave him hanging, always provide back vocals.

The exception to the above is that you can as co-pilot (Chewie to your mate's Han Solo, Goose to his Maverick) start air drums or guitar.

MEN COMMANDMENT IV

Men and Fire
[Thou shalt not come between
a man and his chicken wings]

As a man you must always show little or no respect to a fire. It's there to be tamed by us and to be moulded into whatever we want to use it for. Men respect other men that have a detailed knowledge of fire. Remember when you were young and you were in the presence of a bonfire. Despite the wretched stink of damp leaves, fox shit and hedgehogs, I remember seeing how my normally pretty sane dad was transformed by his bonfire. It scared me as a kid because it made him really odd. Well, odder. Just moving towards him or into his postcode while he was standing guard over it would trigger off some kind of weird primeval guttural cry from him.

GET BACK... FOR GOD'S SAKE, GET BACK...

My mum would give me a look as if to say, 'Don't worry, fire does this to a man.' Once I swore I saw him chanting at it like some sort of dad shaman. I welcomed the day I would become a Bonfire Dad. One winter, when I was 13, I was invited to stand near to his bonfire. Near to, mind, not next to. It was a pure father-son bonding moment. Two men, a fire, and some hedgehogs burning to death. You can't beat that for bonding. I bet even in his dark heart big Darth Vader wishes he'd had a Bonfire Moment with his son Luke. Maybe Darth wouldn't have ended up chopping off his son's hand if they'd bonded over a bonfire and in turn maybe Luke wouldn't have wanted to have sex with his own sister.

SOOT IS NUTRITIOUS

I think these days men's fire fix doesn't come from bonfires but from the king of all things fire... the barbecue. I remember the exact time and place when I got my first barbecue. Talk about rites of passage. This was a real life moment for me. Losing my barbie cherry. You always remember your first. The men working there – sages, really – ushered me in knowing the event was almost too big for me to comprehend. The only other time I have witnessed similar proud looks was when I was first handed my newborn daughter – and to be honest, she didn't even come with burger tongs and a free meat rub sauce. The sales assistants were very happy to see me in the barbecue aisle at first, but I had made the fatal mistake of bringing my wife. Once Mrs O'Connell turned up, those happy smiles turned to venomous stares. I had brought an outsider into their midst.

Anyway, I managed to buy one and bundled it out of the shop before my wife could see the price tag. Once I got it home I prepared for the Big Barbie. Now it's important when preparing a barbecue to follow these rules:

THE BARBIE THREE-STEP

1. When loading up the charcoal, the rule of quantity is this: however much you think you need, times it by three.

2. The instruction booklet you get is also very useful, as a firelighter.

3. Ignore anyone suggesting you don't put the meat on until the flames die down and the charcoal turns white. Soot is nutritious and counts towards your five a day.

Now for the cooking. Well, I say cooking, I mean cremating. No one must come within five feet of the barbecue unless they are collecting food to be eaten or a very good friend (or bringing the chef – you – a drink). Let's get one thing straight: a barbecue is not a democracy. People can't wander up and say things like, 'That piece of chicken looks done, can I have it?' It must be a dictatorship with you at the head of it. I'm no anthropologist but at any sort of barbecue situation, men instantly regress to their caveman days. Any sort of a challenge to our fire-poking capabilities is met with swift retribution:

'Hiya, mate, do you want me to give those steaks a turn?'

'Back the fuck off!'

'I just thought that...'

'Go now. Or I'll impale you with these burger skewers.'

I once saw a horrific sight at a barbecue. My friend had one of those amazing gas ones, where you can actually adjust the temperature, and it had three grills, and 'resting shelves' to keep the cooked meat hot. All the men found themselves migrating towards it like flies to a big dog turd.

Anyway, he went for a quick toilet break and one man, who I didn't really know, stepped up to the barbie and started rearranging the meat. I don't know if he wasn't aware of the rule or maybe he was high on meat fumes. There was a collective sharp intake of breath from the rest of us. He might as well have taken my mate's wife and started humping her on the kitchen floor. I'd like to say what we did then was all band together and burn him alive inside a wicker man, but instead all we did was tut and give him dirty looks. I think my friend got his own back later by giving him all the bits of meat he kept dropping on the floor.

Thou shalt covet thy own barbecue, never another man's.

Ever seen an episode of *Ramsey's Kitchen Nightmares* where he tries to give advice to a man cooking a barbecue? No, and do you know why? Because he'd be murdered before the first ad break.

Back to the Big Barbie preparation. When it comes to sorting out the meat, you only need get three types: chicken, burgers/steaks, and sausages. The chicken should always go on first, because you become obsessed that you might undercook it. This obsession always leads to one result: burnt on the outside, raw on the inside. But that's not a disaster. People can just eat the outsides.

Next on are the burgers. You have two options when buying burgers. The expensive ones that look meaty and gorgeous or the frozen ones that come in packs of 20, that look like shrunken bits of coal when they're cooked. Always go for quantity and remember, by the time they come off the assembly line, everybody's too drunk for their taste buds to work properly. Next up is the forgotten man of barbecues, the sausage. Always buy too many sausages for a barbecue. There's no reason for this but always do it because a barbecue isn't a barbecue unless there's somebody saying 'Anybody want another sausage?' at the end. Often overlooked for its more glamorous meat cousins, you'll find yourself not even putting the sausages on the grill until the fire is well on its way to dying out.

There's one final rule to a barbecue. If it's you who is doing the cooking, you should never feel satisfied at the end. The combination of too much lager on an empty stomach and a burnt red face from the raging heat of the fire should mean that when it's time to feed yourself, you are no longer hungry. But don't feel too sad. Look around your garden. Are there paper plates strewn over your lawn with half-eaten bits of meat on them? Is there somebody eating a pink chicken wing? Is there a bowl of coleslaw, which you've put out as a pathetic attempt at salad, sat on a wallpapering table completely untouched with flies buzzing around it? Is there a lone sausage which has slipped through the grill sitting on the charcoal gazing up at you forlornly? If the answer to any of those questions is 'yes', then, my friend, you have 'done' a barbecue.

MEN COMMANDMENT V

Man Crushes
[Honour and love another man but not in a girly way]

In this age of uncertainties you may wonder to what degree you may admire another man. The lines are very blurred. Why is it OK to go into a pub and say, 'I love the way David Beckham can curl a ball into the top corner of the net,' but not OK to say, 'I love the way David Beckham wears his suits. He can pull off any look effortlessly'?

I'm talking about man crushes and the way you express admiration for other men. It's a minefield but let me explain how you can cross it. A quick look at the excellent website Urban Dictiontionary.com sheds some light on this condition:

Man crush is a very strong feeling that one straight man has for another, bordering on the romantic but not the sexual. It's love all right but not the love that makes you want to get into his pants. It can be stronger than the love between a man and a woman.

WHEN MEN WERE MEN

Now it may just be the fact I'm getting to the age where I'm looking at the world through rose-tinted spectacles but I'm sure that when I was a kid, men could do things. By 'things' I mean fixing the car when it broke down instead of calling out the AA like some sort of mechanical eunuch. By 'things' I mean knowing how to fish, owning a shed, and having at least one friend who had been in the army and who may or may not have seen somebody get 'slotted'. For instance, my dad used to be able to build stuff out of wood and nails. From scratch using some sort of voodoo DIY. It's a symptom of our increasing emasculation that companies market a product called No More Nails. Yes, it does the job just as well – some say even better than nails – but for a man to be a man he needs to be able to bang things in with a hammer.

In my eyes modern man is a pale, diminished version of his former self and it's this distinct lack of a male compass which leads us to form man crushes. They're not crushes in the traditional sexual sense of the word. It's more how we look to other men who have certain talents to be our leaders. It's the mate with a cool job; it's the guy in the office who all the girls like; it's the friend who's really good at football. '*He had trials at Chelsea, you know...*' you find yourself mumbling to your girlfriend as she asks you to justify spending a Friday night with him rather than her. I suppose it's all about projecting the things than you can't do, or can't be, on to other men.

A prime example is the way Richie, Potsie and Ralph looked up to the Fonz. Three nerds adrift in a sea of teenage angst looked to him for guidance. They all wanted to be like him. He rode motorcycles, he was as hard as a brick shithouse, and he was good-looking. He was also an unemployed mechanic who lived in a garage, and liked to hang out with teenage boys, but that's not the point. The primeval urge to bond with and look up to other men was manifesting itself in their devotion to this Alpha 'Fonzie'.

Given the chance, when not procreating, men will always want to hang round with other men as opposed to women.

Modern constraints stop him from doing so. It's only in the second half of the twentieth century that male life has changed. Historically most men would be married by 21 and go out and earn a living and socialise in a world populated mostly by other men, and 'the wife' would stay at home and make house. Now I'm not suggesting for a minute that this was a good thing, but in modern life, men have to spend every waking hour with women. Shopping, visiting relatives, romantic dinners. It's only natural that as time spent with other men has diminished over the years, our affection for them has grown.

Now I imagine a lot of you are sitting at home thinking, Jesus, this guy is crazy. Sure, I like other men, but a crush? Well, just imagine for a moment that you could choose between dating a beautiful woman or hanging around with George Clooney. Conversation with a vapid blonde in an overpriced restaurant or playing poker with George? Pretending to be interested in what she does for a living or listening to George tell a story about how he got it on with three girls in the back of his limo. It's a no-brainer. If the name George featured heavily in your answers just now, welcome to the world of man crushes, my friend.

A CONFESSION

My own man crush, which I've had for years now, is over Jeff
Stelling from *Soccer Saturday*. Every Saturday afternoon I find
myself in awe of his masterful handling of the latest footie results.
If I was as good as him I'd have more listeners to my radio show
and thrash Moyles and Wogan. I want to hang out with him. I
want to be the Wise to his Morecambe. A recurring fantasy of
mine involves Jeff and I holding court in a proper men's boozer.
He's wearing a V-necked sweater with his hairy chest showing,
immaculate Farah slacks and a pair of lovely loafers. He's also
smoking a Hamlet cigarillo – I don't know why, but it adds to his
mystique. Everyone's laughing at our jokes, and jealous of our
blokey banter. Drinks are offered to us left, right and centre from
hangers-on and well-wishers. But suddenly Jeff turns to me and
with a deadly serious look on his face purrs, '*Christian, you might
just be the best friend I've ever had. Well, apart from Chris Kamara,
but sometimes I find the way he laughs annoying. Let's say we blow
this joint. Let's pop down to my shed. I'm going to teach you how to
bang stuff in with a hammer.*'

BUYING A GIFT FOR ANOTHER MAN

Instinctively I would say don't do it. However, in some situations it
is necessary. Women love buying gifts for each other. It's very
important to them and they put in real time and effort. Men don't.
If you really have to buy one, never spend more than 15 minutes
on choosing it. I mean, some of you wouldn't do that for your wife.

I got myself in an awkward situation at Christmas when under my
wife's advice I bought a friend of mine some aftershave. I was

shunned by friends when they found out. I'd broken a code that even I wasn't aware of.

Here are some acceptable Man Gifts for Other Men:

- Alcohol. Always welcome. For instance, if a friend helps you move house or something, you can legally only pay him with beer.

- Cooking knives.

- DVD, not of a new film but a classic. A man's classic with a message. Either a heroic dog giving up his life for his master (*Turner and Hooch*) or men doing incredible things together (*Gladiator*, *The Great Escape*).

- A power tool of some sort. The higher the voltage it runs on the more you value him as a friend.

- The message should always be ironic, as it puts a protective shield over us and stops us from becoming too affectionate to each other.

And one thing men never do is write thank you notes. I don't think I would know what to do if a mate sent me one.

MEN COMMANDMENT VI

Breaking Up with a Mate
[Thou shalt ignore any kind
of confrontation and
hope it goes away]

Breaking up with a mate is actually much harder than with a girlfriend. How do you do it? You can't have the traditional chat about it 'not being you, it's me'. Or the classic 'we can still be friends'. It simply can't happen like that with men. Maybe he didn't offer to help you move house or he's that mate you've had for years but you've drifted apart. I've always found that in every group of friends there's always one member who everybody actually hates and no one knows why they're friends with them. If you're reading this and thinking, bollocks, that's not true, then, my friend, you're the person everybody in the group hates.

Women dump friends all the time. Just look at the Sugababes. How many times have you come home to find your wife having tea in the kitchen with a woman you were sure she said she hated just a week before? But with men it's very different.

There's never actually a call to say I don't want to see you any more. You don't go round to his house and dump all the things he's lent you on his front lawn. What you do is simply ignore him. It's a classic man gambit and can also be used for many other things. When we fell out with Saddam Hussein it would have cost us a lot less if instead of bombing the shit out of Iraq, we simply erased his number from our phone. It would have hurt him much more than a laser-guided bomb if he'd found out we'd gone to the pub with Iran, Jordan and Syria and not invited him.

Ignoring people and/or painful events is the perfect way of dealing with them. Admittedly this method has

its downsides, because you might meet them in social situations. If for instance you find yourself at the pub and the 'dumpee' is there, a policy of total ignorance should be adopted. Luckily men are always too self-conscious to say anything as girly as 'Why didn't you return my call?' so they'll just pretend that nothing has happened as well, which is good. So a lot of the time, the whole issue can be avoided, but deep down you both know what happened. Occasionally you'll catch them giving you a look that says: 'YOU FUCKING DUMPED ME!'

If you do need an excuse, always make it about your mobile phone. Along the lines of:

'So you say you rang me last night? Sorry, got a new phone and I didn't have time to transfer the SIM across...'

The issue of dumping mates leads on to cheating on them. This is acceptable in certain situations. By cheating I mean going out with one mate but not asking another. This is usually when you have a pair of tickets for a gig or a football match and you have to choose the friend you most want to take. Sometimes it's by accident and you assumed your friend was calling him, and by the time you make it to the pub it's too late and there's no point calling him. This is why the World Cup is only once every four years.

Men are piss-poor at organising things.

Sometimes it can be because you don't want to bring a mate to a social situation that doesn't suit his character. Sometimes it's because he falls into one of the following categories:

THE TIGHTWAD

We all know somebody that is so tight his arse squeaks when he walks. They are often not invited to things. Not a lot of people know this, but there was a thirteenth disciple of Jesus called Terry. He was written out of the Gospels in the end because he didn't get invited to the Last Supper. The last time they invited him out, at the wedding at Cannae, he embarrassed the whole group.

'Terry, pay up, mate, it's 15 denarii each.'

'Hang on, I didn't have a starter and I didn't have any alcohol. Why should I have to pay as much as everyone else?'

'What does it matter – no one's paying for booze anyway. Jesus turned all the water into wine again.'

'All right but I'm not tipping.'

The rule is, if there's limited places on a mates outing, the guy who says 'I'm not getting shots' when it's his turn to buy a round isn't getting an invitation.

THE TOPPER

You know the man I'm talking about. Anytime somebody's telling a story, his has to be bigger and better. He often starts his stories with 'I remember the time', 'I've got a better one that that' or 'Ha! That's nothing.'

You've been paintballing? He was in the SAS.

You went out last night and had seven pints? He had eight. And a tequila.

THE DEPRESSING DRUNK

We all like a drink, but there's always one friend who takes it that one step too far. By day he's a lovely fellow but after a couple he becomes sullen and aggressive. Whether he's complaining about the wife who's left him or the boss at work, he's just no fun to be around. Some people just bring everybody down.

'Hey, cheer up, let's put some music on the jukebox.'

'Music. We used to listen to music before she left me...'

Some people just can't be helped, which is why sometimes it's just best if they stay at home.

I'm not saying it's OK to leave mates out in the cold, but it doesn't hurt once in a while. We can learn a great deal from *The Godfather*. Michael had to deal with his brother Fredo. I'm not suggesting the shooting of annoying mates and family members or taking fishing trips with them. I'm just saying that sometimes a little action is needed.

If you have seen the brilliant documentary *Touching the Void* you'll know that difficult decisions have to be made. Two mates were climbing the Peruvian Andes when one has to cut the rope which his mate is hanging on to for dear life, and save himself. What I am saying is if your mate doesn't offer to help you move, cut the rope.

MEN COMMANDMENT VII

Friend-Making
[Thou shalt not like anyone of whom thy wife or girlfriend says, 'You'll really like him']

Maybe it's in our man DNA but after a certain age we almost give up making new best mates. A man has all the friends he needs at the age of 28. Sometimes you might make a friend at work, but you always keep him separate from your proper mates.

If someone tries to make friends with you, there is a feeling that you should say, 'Sorry, mate, all positions are filled at the moment.' It seems like too much hassle to start a new friendship sometimes. Women love making new friends all the time. We don't. It's just too much effort.

Nevertheless it is necessary to make new friends when we're thrust into unfamiliar situations, like a new job, or having to go to a social function made up exclusively of your wife's or partner's friends.

THE NEW BOY

We've all been that new guy in the office who desperately wants to be seen as a fun guy to hang out with. Resist the temptation to do this. Too much keenness and enthusiasm is a red-light warning to men. Women are much better at doing this than we are. They can make friends in any situation. If aliens ever land on this planet, we shouldn't send the government to meet them, but rather a group of girls from the accounts department to make friends with the alien's wives. We'd have an Intergalactic Peace Accord within weeks. Unless the alien wives are better-looking, funnier and smarter than them, in which case they'd close ranks and beat them to death with their stilettos.

With men it's different. It's almost like other men immediately assume we're arseholes and we have to prove otherwise. My advice is to bide your time. Play it cool. Wait for the right moment to make the right play to show that you're not going to be a liability down the pub. Conversation starters like 'Did you see *Dancing On Ice* last night?' are a definite no-no.

Humour is a good ice-breaker. It might be a funny off-the-cuff one-liner but not *too* funny as every office has the dreaded Colin Hunt type, constantly trying too hard to be funny. He is also the one who keeps forwarding painfully unfunny email attachments (always having 'FW' in the subject heading and 'Check This out !!')

Ease into the office conversations, never butt into them. Don't be the guy who comes in with a:

'Who's that you're talking about, then?'

Only to be bitch-slapped with the:

'Oh... you don't know them...'

If those words are ever uttered to you, then you might as well type your letter of resignation there and then, because you ain't never getting asked down the pub on a Friday night.

You can't really initiate a night out unless you've been given 'made man' status within the office. Remember how happy Joe Pesci was in *Goodfellas* when he got his button but then they killed him because he was trying to move up the ranks too fast? (Or maybe it was because they had seen how annoying he was in *Lethal Weapon* 2.) Don't be that guy. Be confident but not forceful. Don't be the guy hovering outside the circle in the pub or round the kettle. If you're lurking outside the circle because no one will let you in, get in there because no one's going to invite you in.

Make sure you've done your homework too and know who played last night and what was on TV. Never ask, 'Sorry, what football match? Who was playing?' You might as well just turn up crying and ask where the loos are as you've wet yourself. I'm not saying it's easy. Every radio station I have worked for, they always hate the new breakfast show DJ. Or maybe it's just me they disliked.

Once you get over the first hurdles and aren't perceived as some sort of weirdo, you need to take it to the next level. It's very hard to do this as you might be received as some sort of predatory homosexual. The phrase 'Do you mind if I call you?' might as well mean 'Do you mind I if put your hot salty balls in my mouth?' if it's uttered from one man to another. It's best just to give him your phone number and let him make his mind up rather than asking for his. Or put the word 'beer' in the request and you're on safe ground. Say, 'Do you want to go for a beer sometime?' and you're signalling to him that your intentions are on the level. Leave out the beer – 'Do you want to go out some time?' – and you're back in hot salty ball territory.

YOU'D REALLY LIKE HIM...

Unfortunately sometimes we're forced to make new friends by wives and girlfriends. They often get obsessed with doing stuff as couples, which no man likes but habitually has to endure.

'You'd really like him. He likes American TV shows too.'

The barriers go up right away when we hear this. I bet Harold Shipman liked sport too. Doesn't mean I want to share a takeaway with him. Sometimes they are so forceful it's almost like they're whoring us out.

Frequently you get the 'I met Sharon's husband Mark. Really funny guy – you'd get on well with him. Thought I'd invite them round.'

'YOU DID WHAT? ANOTHER MAN INTO MY CAVE WHO I DON'T KNOW? THE ROOM'S SPINNING. I FEEL SICK...'

And when they come round they always do that thing where they leave the two of you alone together, so you have to make conversation. It's actually against the laws of man physics for those types of relationships to work. You just can't put men together like that and expect it to work. They're too busy being angry at their partner's betrayal to make friends. Then there will be the attempt at getting some banter going.

'So Karen tells me you strangle kittens for a living – how's all that going?'

Then, if you manage to actually get some half semblance of a conversation going, you will have to survive the military-style debrief within seconds of the front door closing. 'What were you talking about?'

So many times I have walked into the 'he loves all the TV shows you do' trap and then you have to make small talk with a very dull man who works in IT or manages hedge funds and has halitosis and *who does not like the same things as me*. He's never seen a single episode of *The Sopranos* or *The West Wing*. But the trap has been set... SNAP. The worst part of it is the chat you get when they've left, or on the way home. 'You never even gave him a chance. Why are you so anti-social?' The best thing to do in these situations, and I'm not saying it's ideal, guys, is to lie. Tell them that he kept making racist jokes, or that he said your wife looked older than she was, or that he thinks Adolf Hitler was very misunderstood. Anything you want, but just make sure you smear that man's name enough so that he never darkens your door again.

Sometimes, it has to be said, I have actually made some great friends this way. (Throughout this book I have frequently contradicted myself. Proving once again that men are full of crap.) Then it's even more fraught as you find yourself liking the guy and wanting him to like you. Suddenly you fear *you* are the dull man that you dread being stuck with who smells. You frantically search your killer man chat topics hard drive to stimulate some scintillating man talk. He may not like sport so you play down your obsession with it, or he may like cars so you pretend you know what the hell a catalytic converter does. (Converts catalytics, right?)

I'll give you a lifeline you can use should you ever find yourself struggling to entertain a man you actually like. I have put this question to every man I have interviewed over the last few years and without exception they love it. A TV show was even made after hearing me use it. It is simple. It contains two things men love a lot: TV and nostalgia. The question is: If anything was to happen to you, which TV detective would you want to solve your murder?

Will Ferrell said Helen Mirren as Jane Tennyson from *Prime Suspect*. The phrase he used was, 'She can still bring it, right?' Bon Jovi and Noel Gallagher said Columbo. Quentin Tarantino said Gil Grissom, Seagal said Jack Bauer from 24. It has all the components that make it a question for men to devote serious brain time to. Use it well, my friends.

MEN COMMANDMENT VIII
Dating Etiquette
[Thou shalt not lust
after a mate's sister]

This really is a tricky one. There are two main areas to be dealt with here. Going out with a friend's ex and going out with a friend's relative.

First up, going out with a mate's ex. The acceptable period of time for approaching a mate's ex-girlfriend is at least 100 years. If this all goes to plan you must never speak of your relationship with this girl to your mate. Ever. Phrases like 'You never said she was amazing in bed... We even did the Chinese wheelbarrow last night' can often open up a can of worms and flying fists. The acceptable exchange would be more like this:

Your friend:	How's it going with Susie?
You:	All right.
Your friend:	Good.
You:	Yup.

It can also happen the other way around. Maybe a friend of yours starts dating an ex. The key thing is to never show your feelings. Inside you may be heartbroken that your one true love is now sleeping with one of your friends and every time you see them together it feels like your heart is being slashed by tiny razor blades, with lasers on. But you must never show them that. Think of Patrick Swayze in *Roadhouse* when he's in casualty getting stitches and refuses any anaesthetic. The nurse falls immediately in love with him as she recognises him from *Dirty Dancing*. Inside the Sway was hurting but he didn't so much as wince. Be like Swayze. It's better to let it gnaw away inside you and reduce you to a gibbering wreck of stomach ulcers than let your friend see your emotional side.

The second and most lethal area is that of dating another man's sister. If you've been for a beer with a man more than once then forget about going out with his sister. It's just not worth the hassle, unless your three best friends are called Bobby Jolie, Darren Moss and Dean Evangelista. Men who do this are marked for life with a *Manwa*. A Man Fatwa. It's harder to shake off than a bad credit rating.

At my best friend's wedding his sister said to my wife, 'Christian is the only one of my brother's mates who never tried it on with me...' I cannot tell you how proud my wife was, and how slightly disappointed in myself I was.

If you're still determined, take the last smart check before going any further. Have a... How can I put it in a grown-up and smart book like this without being crude and again ruining my chances of being in Richard and Judy's Book Club? You should try 'relaxing in the gentleman's way'. Then see how you feel about her in the morning. To be honest, this is a tactic that works in most cases.

MEN COMMANDMENT IX

Lending and Borrowing [Thou shalt not covet thy mate's box set of *The Sopranos*]

The phrase 'Neither a borrower nor a lender be' is a very apt one when it comes to men. In an ideal world we would give a borrowed item back within three working days like a DVD rental, but we rarely do.

When calculating the proper duration of borrowing, a simple equation is needed. If he borrows a power drill and says he will return it within a week, myltiply that amount of time by twelve. If you borrow something that needs refuelling, like a car or a lawnmower, then you must always return it with the minimum amount of petrol in it.

NEVER RE-LEND, MY FRIEND

The biggest rule you can break in the world of borrowing is the re-lend. You borrow a film from 'friend A'. A week later 'friend B' visits your house and sees the film and asks if he can borrow it. You're unsure but he says he'll have it back within a few days, which as we know from the aforementioned equation means three months. Another week later A visits B's house and sees the film. He says, 'Hey, I've got that, it's good, isn't it?' and B says, 'Yeah, it's great, Christian lent it to me.' A immediately knows that you've been lending out his property and vows never to let you borrow anything ever again.

Never get caught out in a re-lend, my friends, as it's a surefire way to get cut out of the borrowing circle. Another crime is to borrow a film or a box set and never get round to watching it. You can often see the hurt on a friend's face when they ask you what you thought and you give a vague noncommittal answer. They know. They know. If your buddy gives you *Band of Brothers* or *The Wire*, it's like he's giving you a part of him. You are not rejecting the DVD box set of *24*, you are rejecting your mate. It is more of a man slur than saying his wife or girlfriend is really carrying some weight around her arse these days.

Men Commandment: if you borrow a DVD box set of:

Band of Brothers

Bilko

The Wire

The Sopranos

The West Wing

24

you must watch it all

If this means taking some time off work or taking a relationship break, so be it. And you don't just have to watch it; you then have to partake in discussions at length about the meaning of the ducks in *The Sopranos*.

Borrowing money is also a tricky subject. Say you lend a friend a tenner, in today's terms a relatively small sum of money. The next week you're out with them again. Do you wait for the slim chance that they will remember they owe you money or do you ask for it back and risk looking like a tightarse in front of everybody? What you should never try and do is shoehorn it into conversation.

'I'm reading *A Tale of Two Cities* at the moment by Charles Dickens. If you're not aware of his work, he also appears on the ten-pound note, which reminds me, can I have that tenner you owe me?'

The best idea is to simply ask him to lend you a tenner. Then he will probably ask you to lend him a tenner the following week and so on and so forth until you get to the point where no one knows who owes who what.

It is also generally accepted that if you lend a mate anything less than a note then it should never have to be repaid. Just a nod and 'you get my curry' is fine.

Items such as tools come under a different set of rules. You must respect another man's tools as if they were deities. You use them for the job at hand and then immediately hand them back, even if it's two in the morning.

'CAN I TRY SOME OF YOURS?'

Never ever lean over and try a bit of your mate's food. It's the ultimate act of disrespect. Tony Soprano started a gang war when rival boss Phil Leonardo did it to him. I fully understand that sometimes, when the food comes out, a horrible realisation creeps over you that you've ordered the wrong dish and your friend's looks much much tastier. Order envy. It happens. You see the next table being brought a fantastic dish while yours looks like crap. Hold fast though. You should never ask to sample another man's food under any circumstances. The only exception is pizza, which is helpfully divided into slices.

MEN COMMANDMENT X

Man Talk
(Thou shalt always take the piss at every opportunity)

Men love winding each other up. Pushing each other's boundaries and hoping they will snap. Goading them about ex-girlfriends, football teams, sexuality, their mum, their car.

There are no limits to what we are allowed to say to each other. What some men do to each other would be classed as mental torture under the Geneva Convention. Nothing is sacred or sacrosanct.

One good source of abuse is the allocation of a nickname: this must be given at the earliest stage of any friendship. The person in question may not choose it. You can't all sit down together and work out what name will suit him. It must be based on a horrible incident, a disgusting facial feature, an unfounded rumour about their mother.

Once, on a drunken night out in Edinburgh, one of my friends very nearly killed himself. In a vain attempt to get a taxi, he jumped out in front of one as it was hurtling down the street. (I know, I know, not very clever.) He soon realised that this was a mistake. Somehow powered by the Ready Brek glow of drunken goodness, his addled mind made the calculation that he didn't have enough time to safely jump out of the way. So he decided to try and jump over the taxi,, judging that because of its velocity it would pass under him and he could land safely on the other side. A truly awesome idea of unbelievable stupidity that could easily have killed him and the cabbie.

He got about two feet off the ground and not being in any way, shape or form gymnastically endowed, he got bounced over the car's windscreen and roof. We all rushed over. The taxi skidded to a halt, the driver frozen in fear of what lay in a heap behind him. A crumpled little ginger Irishman. He opened his eyes, gave the Fonzie double thumbs-up, and started laughing. A nickname was born. To this day we still call him 'Hooper' as a homage to the great Burt Reynolds stuntman film.

Piss-taking is as natural as breathing for any group of men larger than three. It's always funny, when you see a tramp, to claim he's one of your friend's parents. Fashion is always a good one too.

'Bob, the 1930s called.'

'What?'

'They want their jacket back.'

That one gets better with repetition.

YOUR MATE ON THE PHONE

You must never, repeat *never*, hold a phone conversation with another man that lasts longer than 60 seconds. There are three and only three stages in a phone call between men:

- **STAGE ONE:** Tell him why you are ringing; state your

business. You don't have one? Just ringing for no reason? Do you actually have a penis or large pendulous breasts?

'Just calling up to say she's left me.'

- **STAGE TWO:** Say what you want from him.

' ...and taken the car so gonna need a lift to the game.'

- **STAGE THREE:** Wait for his reply, which should only comprise of one or two possible words. Yes or no. That's it. Or a grunt or mumble.

'Sure, fine.'

Or

'nng'

Hang up.

With the advent of texting men have found an even better way to communicate. It's cold, impersonal and doesn't involve any talking. Perfect.

I hope these commandments have been as useful to you as they have been to me over the years. If you ever find yourself in a sticky situation and are not quite sure what to do, look back at these hallowed rules and regulations and consult them, nodding once in a while like a wise old sage.

And if you ever find yourself in a sticky situation that this book hasn't covered, I'm more than happy to try to help you. Just don't approach me at a urinal.

I taught you better than that.

I ASKED MY LOVELY LISTENERS TO SEND ME THEIR OWN MEN COMMANDMENTS ON TWITTER

I have to be honest and warn you that some are from ladies and some are from quite frankly scary people, but thanks to everyone who got involved.

Sometimes I have allowed more than one as they were so good, some aren't strictly commandments but who cares right? What man ever stuck to a set of rules?

1. Yeffor@The_OC

Why do guys refuse to take any medication if man flu is so bad? And 'men should not wear ugg boots' must be a commandment!

2. tomswenchie@The_OC

No man should ever do the John Travolta point-to-the-ceiling-point-to-the-floor dance move; also that one from Pulp Fiction.

3. braveheartbri@The_OC

Real men should never use a brolly no matter how wet he'll get. Oh and never call an umbrella a brolly.

4. cyclingeurope@The_OC

It's every man's right to watch the footie results in the TV section of House of Fraser when shopping with the missus.

5. tgnipper@The_OC

A man should never go for a number 2 without reading material... And he should take 10 minutes as a minimum length of time.

6. jovijedi@The_OC

Men should never be seen reading glossy mags such as Hello unless it is to criticize celebs such as "thought their house would be bigger".

7. GIANT71@The_OC

Never ask a women her sexual fantasy, men just cannot compete with the depravity a women can conjure up.

8. russelmes@The_OC

A man must reach his desired petrol filling cost with the least pump tweaks possible. A petrol bullseye is a manly pinnacle.

9. Luna07@The_OC

If men want to drink copious amounts of alcohol and act like a cocky 14-year-old adolescent, please do not come home and expect sex.

10. Luna07@The_OC

Men should never fart and waft it towards your face. You think funny, we think "I can't believe I sleep with him".

I NOW HAVE TO PICK THE WINNER AND IT'S BEEN HARD BUT IT'S THIS ONE...

Chardo301@The_OC

No man should ask another man to open a jar for him.
Except if he has lost both arms and even then he should try with his feet first.

INDEX

Ali, Muhammad 165, 230-1, 236
America's Next Top Model 7, 243
Animal Face Off 129
Animal Hospital 6, 67, 84
Animal House 174
Apollo space programme 48-9
apologies, without knowing why 7,
    83-4
Aquarians, cause of fight 70
Art Attack 36
A-Team 88, 198, 219, 224-5, 257

Baird, John Logie 46-7
barbecue 8, 37, 181, 214, 217 260-3
Bauer, Jack 8, 50, 98, 169, 172, 196,
    201, 228, 278
beer, ancient Egyptians and 37-8
Benn, Nigel 181
Blackadder Goes Forth 181
blue, duck-egg 8, 106
Bodie & Doyle 5, 201-2, 254
Bonaparte, Napoleon 44-5
Bond, James 8, 79, 185, 196, 227-8
Bono 250, 253
Bourne Ultimatum 50, 200
Bourne, Jason 79, 228
Butch Cassidy and the Sundance Kid
    193-5

Caine, Michael 154, 184, 232, 244
candles, scented 6, 242
Canoe man 167-170
cars, naming of them 140, 159-60
cards 99-101
cats:
    and skips 12-13
    as judgemental little shits 57
    cleaning of them 147
    or dogs 7, 126
cheese grater, use of across
    scrotum 3
chicken, the cooking of 8, 37, 214,
    261-2

Churchill, Winston 221-2, 228, 236
Clarks commandos 13
Columbo 51, 125, 223-6, 278
condoms, proper use of 79
contraceptive pill 47
Costner, Kevin 175
Couch, Kent 170-3

dancing 20, 153, 154, 178
Dancing on Ice 6, 109, 153-4, 274
Darwin Awards 62
Dastardly, Dick 226-7, 236
dating etiquette 278-80
Davies, Dickie 152
Dempsey and Makepeace 20
denim, low-slung 9, 50, 216
De Niro, Robert 22, 199-200, 234
Desperate Housewives 79, 244
Die Hard: With A Vengeance
    196-7
dinner ladies 17
discos, school 20-1
dogs 8, 57, 67, 97, 117, 125, 239,
    241, 257
Dr Who 76, 181
Dumb and Dumber 186-7

Eastwood, Clint 23, 173
Einstein, Albert 32
Eubank, Chris 181-2

Fatal Attraction 162
Ferguson, Sir Alex 109
Field of Dreams 175-6
Flintstone, Wilma, sex with 205
Flintstones, The 204-5
Fonze 29
Friends 203-4, 241

garden chair, as flying machine
    170-2
Gibson, Mel 125, 190-1,
Godfather, The 179

Godfather: Part III, The 5, 179, 193, 272,
Goodfellas 60, 184, 275
Grant, Russell 70
Great Escape, The 23, 53, 55, 268
Grylls, Bear 12
Gunpowder Plot 42

Hackman, Gene 220, 244
Happy Days 35
Harry Potter 5
Hasselhoff, David 229-230, 236
Henry VIII, King 40-1, 222-3, 227, 236
Hitler, Adolf 31, 47, 277
Hollywood 183-200
Hoover, Henry 146-8

iMan 214, 215
Indiana Jones and the Last Crusade 195

Kirk, Captain James T. 76, 207-11, 256
Knightrider 108, 229, 252, 254

Last Tango in Paris 184
Leia, Princess, in golden chains 5
lemon barley squash 28, 29
Lethal Weapon 125, 190-1, 275
Livingstone, Doctor 74
Loggins, Kenny 48, 206, 244

Magnum PI 202, 254
Man Card, The 54, 216
Man Shui 240
Manwidth 70, 133-4
Mastermind 184
McCartney, Sir Paul 35
McQueen, Steve 53, 55, 184
Mears, Ray 12, 231-2
men:
  and being neutered 58-9
  and bullshit 66, 68, 77, 112, 114
  and DIY 141-3, 151
  and Facebook 71
  and farting 134-5
  and flu 137-9

and gifts 71, 158-9, 267-8
and hair loss 39-40
and loose change 156
and lucky pants 8, 135-6
and musicals 9, 16-17, 129, 131-2, 154
and nicknames 154-5
  nudging 245-7
  problem solving 62-6
  shopping 34, 58, 62, 79-81,123
  speedos 238
  splitting bills 89
  tears 81, 173-5
  texting 71-3, 286, 73-4
  toilet time 132
  washing car 252-4
  world without 214-16
men and women, genetic differences 83-159
microwave oven 32, 33, 49
Midnight Run 199-200
Million Dollar Baby 171, 173
Minder 72, 205-6
Morissette, Alanis 162-4
movies:
  top five man tears 175-81
  top ten guy 185-200
Mr T 178, 219, 224-5, 235, 236

Olympics 38, 91

pants, magical Dad 13
PE 14-16
penis:
  and the first step towards civilisation 36
  and slow dance demonstrations 20-1
  another man's 78, 257-8
  detachable 214
  measuring 18
Picard, Jean-Luc 209-11
Pitt, Brad 61, 234
Police Academy 4
pornographic magazines 19-20
Porridge 212
Poseidon Adventure, The 220
Prescott, John 166

Presley, Elvis 16-17, 47-8
Professionals, The 5, 96, 201-2

remote control 5, 32, 51, 137, 238, 239, 242-5
rites of passage 11-29
rock and roll 47, 51
Rockford Files, The 20
Rocky III 3
Rocky IV 6, 176
Rocky V 178
Rocky VI 178
Rogers, Kenny 48, 165
Rolf's Cartoon Club 36, 84
Rubble, Betty, having sex with 205

Seagal, Steven 4, 48, 51, 131, 154, 184, 232-236, 278, 288
Sex and the City 3, 66, 78, 79, 104-5, 129, 168, 182, 216
Shawshank Redemption, The 178-9
sirloin, origin of 42
Sinatra, Frank 234-6
Smeaton, John 220
Soccer Saturday 267
Sons of the Desert 197
soot, nutritional value of 260
Soprano, Tony 31, 139, 185, 226, 283
Sopranos, The 31, 72, 132, 181, 277, 280, 282
Spencer, Percy 32, 49
St John's Ambulance Brigade 28-9
Stand by Me 81
Star Trek 76, 207-10
Star Wars 5
Starsky and Hutch 5
Stelling, Jeff 168, 267
Stewart, Robert 148
stink eye 55, 116-17, 124
Strictly Come Dancing 6-7, 153-4
superheros 150-1
Swingers 192-3
Sykes, Brian 213

Tango & Cash 197-8
tardis 76
television:
  emotional 181-3

42-inch plasma 6, 126
  glorification of man and 200-12
  invention of 46
  men will watch almost anything on 129-30
  Saturday night 6-7
Tennant, David 76, 181
Terminator 2 220
toilet etiquette 6, 7, 248-51
Top Cat 226
Top Gear 80
Top Gun 179, 187-8, 212
trails, snail 18-20
trousers, Stay Press 14, 21, 29
Tudors, The 40-1
Twentieth Century 46-9
24 72, 170, 206, 278, 281, 282,

Wacky Races 47, 227
Webber, Andrew Lloyd 50, 90, 132
West Wing, The 174, 181, 282
women:
  and bathroom products 131-2
  and eBay 139
  and naming men 159-60
  and naming things that shouldn't be named 159-60
  and sleeping 123
  and sport 108-9
  and their hawklike visions 110-11
  and thinking 6, 118-20
  and weddings 155-6
  conversation 55, 95
  emotional 161
  friendships 59, 61, 68, 69, 269, 273
  shopping 34, 79
  viciousness of 60-1
world, without men 214-15
wrestling, as diplomatic solution 41
Wyman, Bill 257

X Factor 171

Y chromosome 213

Zulu 154

ACKNOWLEDGEMENTS

I always wonder who reads this bit. I always do and wonder is he really thankful or just doing it to save buying a thank you present or even worse send a thank you card. Whatever. I do actually have a few people I have to thank. Without these people this book would have never have been blah blah blah....look it's cheaper than a gift.

Claire Kingston is the person who made the decision that will ultimately make her unemployable; she commissioned me to do this book in the first place. Thanks, sucker, I've got the cash. Thanks also to all the other lovely ladies and lucky few men at HarperCollins. Andy Hipkiss my agent went through hell while I was writing this book. Having to hear my ill-thought-out ideas over cold beers. Thanks. Though he does use hand moisturiser so is part of the problem with men right now. Martin Toseland was the editor and had the devil's job trying to keep my wandering mind on track and had to politely give me notes suggesting that maybe 27 pages on Captain Kirk was a tad too much. You were wrong. He also noticed the number of references to the film *The Great Escape* in the book.

I also want to thank my mates who have inspired me. Phil, Kevin, Sully in Afghanistan, Brian, Roque and the Green Man pub. And Mr Stella Artois.

And the kind people at imdb.com who helped answer my questions about the best movies for men and cast valuable insight into the life and times of Steven Seagal.

I also thank the tens of people who tune in to my radio show. I owe you and love you. Thanks for still listening even when yet another link goes out not fully thought out.

Dad, the first man to really show me that we are nuts. I'm still sorry about throwing up in your car that time.

There are three very special people I want to thank. Without them, there would be no book. They are Ruby and Lois, my daughters. Sorry I wasn't around so much for the few months I was writing this. Dad was busy saving mankind.

And Sarah my wife. You know why. I'm not putting it in print as you may then be entitled to some of the profits.

THE CHRISTIAN
O'CONNELL SHOW.
WEEKDAYS WHEN
YOU WAKE UP.

THAT LEAVES YOU THE
REST OF THE DAY TO GROW UP.

DISCOVER REAL MUSIC
ON 105.8FM · ON 1215AM · DAB

Absolute.
absoluteradio.co.uk